Blessed With Brain Damage

Marisa Scott

Blessed With Brain Damage, Copyright © 2024 by Marisa Scott

All rights reserved.

No portion of this book may be reproduced in any form without written permission from the publisher or author, except as permitted by U.S. copyright law.

THE HOLY BIBLE, NEW INTERNATIONAL VERSION®, NIV® Copyright © 1973, 1978, 1984, 2011 by Biblica, Inc.® Used by permission. All rights reserved worldwide.

I'd like to dedicate this to my beloved R's & J's who inspired and motivated me along this journey: ReRe, JoePa, Jim, Reagan, and Julia.

To the angel who I've had working overtime on far too many occasions, ReRe, aka Mom. You left us all too soon, but I feel your love and prayers daily, especially as I look up to the heavens for your motherly wisdom and protection. You continue to surround me with beautiful rainbows, and in life, you modeled for me the faith and strength I needed every step of this journey. I miss you.

To JoePa, for telling me you wouldn't write this with me or for me. Instead, as always, you have provided your unconditional love, support, and the tools to get me on my way. As my best Dad, you have always been in my corner, and as usual, you were right to let me "do it myself." Thank you for introducing me to faith, leading and living in faith and laying the groundwork I needed all along the way and being the role model of selflessness, service, and humility that you are. I am grateful beyond measure.

To Jim, my love, my rock, and the most handsome of all my doctors for enduring all the challenges along our broken road. Thank you for believing in me, and in us. I wouldn't want any other co-pilot, teammate, or gourmet chef.

To my greatest accomplishments in this world—Julia & Reagan, my brave, faith-filled, beautiful, spectacular girls for giving me purpose and bringing me so much joy. Let this book serve as a reminder that you are loved to the moon and back and you are stronger than you know. Remember that all along the twists and turns, ups and downs, and trials you may encounter on the path God has laid before you, there are many blessings to be found. If your road seems broken at times, I will be your roadside assistance always. I have so much faith in you girls and all the amazing things you are going to bring to this world—stay awesome!

    I couldn't have done this without all of you.

Blessed With Brain Damage

Risa Scott

A Beautifully Blessed and Sometimes Broken Road—My Honest Disclaimer

Writing this book has long been a bucket list passion project for me. I wanted to do this so that I could easily pass along a message of faith, hope, and positivity to anyone, especially for those who might struggle with similar issues. Most importantly, though, I wanted to document my journey so that my brave, bold, and beautiful daughters might someday be able to refer to when in need of a reminder of the incredible and inherited strength that lies within them whenever they may face trials of any kind.

It's amazing I've been able to write about my life's journey considering I can't recall so many of the miles traveled along the way. However, being able to tell the story of the broken but so very blessed road that God planned for me has finally come to fruition. From experiencing the joys of surmounting the most daunting of challenges to suffering the devastating plummet of hitting the lowest of rock bottom lows. Brain damage and all, I am so very honored to share what I can remember and, more importantly, share the message of faith and optimism I've gained from times of struggle in hopes that it leaves a positive impact on you, my much-appreciated reader.

Some of you, as you read this, especially if you were lucky enough to be in my inner circle and receive a copy, may think to yourself as you read, "Hmm, this wasn't what I was expecting." Or "For going to an Ivy League school, she isn't that great of a writer...terrible grammar, subject-verb agreement is way off, run-on sentences, and my goodness, can she please get a grip on her use of passive voice? WAAAAY too much of this faith stuff, too." Well, guess what...

a) I wasn't an English major, and my goal is not/has not ever been to write a New York Times best seller.

b) It's not your story, it's mine.

3) Can't say you haven't been warned upfront regarding the whole "brain damage" thing; I'll get to the part about lost files and pathways later.

M) Did I mention brain damage?

e) Brain-damaged but not entirely humorless if you didn't catch that.

Ultimately, I know who and what I am at the end of the day. If I have disappointed you or you are dissatisfied, know that I tried. Can't hit a home run or even get a base hit if you don't dare to take the swing. And try taking that swing with one eye shut while you're at it. That's akin to writing a full-length retrospective memoir with the piece of your brain controlling memory retention and recall having been removed.

In writing this, I feel like I am continuing to serve God's plan as it was laid out for me. (He received an early edition and, rumor has it, He enjoyed it thoroughly). I am proud of all the twists and turns this story took me on and will now take you on as well. So, pull up a chair. Enjoy the ride...but maybe put on a seatbelt...this story has some rocky turns and bumps along the way.

A Brief Introduction

My name is Risa Scott, and this is the story God created for me. In case you couldn't tell by the title of this book, my faith is a huge part of my life and God will feature prominently in my story. My goal is not to preach or proselytize but to tell my story in the hope that it will inspire and encourage others, no matter where they are on their journey.

From the moment we're born we travel our own unique path. Each of us has a story to tell about our journeys, our struggles, and our triumphs. It is through these paths we walk, the journeys of our lives, and the stories we live that we are best able to connect with the world and with the people we meet.

While it can be tempting to judge ourselves based on the things we have done or not done, what we have accomplished or left incomplete, the truth is that our lives are defined by the God who created us and who has orchestrated every aspect of our lives.

God genuinely has an intriguing sense of humor sometimes, placing things, events, and struggles all along our paths with purpose even if we don't know it at the time. Whether it is amazingly huge milestones or simply small baby steps in the right direction, each step we take serves as another word written in the story of our lives. God, as the great author and perfecter of all things, knows exactly what He is doing, and with each stroke of the pen, He is creating a masterpiece in each of us.

Because of this, it is important that we wholeheartedly lean into the beauty of His artistry and accept that even when our story is difficult and painful, God is moving it forward with a precision and exactness only He could do. No matter the ups and downs, victories and triumphs, without question our path is ultimately unfolding step by step with purpose.

No matter the story He has created for you and the journey you are on, your story is worth telling. By sharing the story about your own miles traveled, mountains hiked, and valleys explored along the way, you can give hope to others by letting them know they are not alone in this world. Collectively, feeling less alone, we may be able to learn from each other's successes as well as missteps.

I'm honored to share my story with you and hope it will inspire and encourage you no matter where you are on your own journey.

Foundations in Faith

My given name is Marisa, but I was almost named after my mother, Marie. My mother loved her name, but her mother and grandmother were also named Marie. She wanted to name me Marie as well, but she thought that people would then start using adjectives to differentiate between so many of the various Maries, and inevitably, she feared ending up being designated either "Old Marie," "Big Marie," or "Fat Marie." My parents had a very good friend whose name was Marisa, and they thought it was a beautiful iteration of the family name. The rest is history. No need for any of the feared Marie monikers after all. And if anything, my mom was more like the "Bossy Marie!"

I am married to a handsome orthopedic surgeon, Jim, and the luckiest mama ever to the greatest lights in my life, my two incredible daughters, Reagan and Julia. I am an unashamed and avid fan of the Philadelphia Phillies, have an Ivy League bachelor's degree in business, and am blessed to have celebrated eleven years of sobriety from alcoholism. Perhaps one of the most defining things about me, though, besides all of these wonderful things, is that I have epilepsy and have survived two brain surgeries.

Surviving brain surgery is mostly thanks to my excellent surgeons' diligence and careful tinkering with my brain. However, the true reason I am able to continue taking each step on the path set before me is because of God's grace and my deep-rooted faith. Faith that my parents introduced me to at an early age.

I was born and raised in a devoutly Catholic home. Both my parents went to Catholic school for high school and college. My brother and I made all our sacraments, attended regular Sunday Mass, and celebrated every religious holiday with a genuine appreciation for God as our higher power and moral compass.

Despite being raised in a devout home and coming to know Christ at a young age, I didn't gain a deeper understanding of what it meant to fully trust in and follow God until later in my life. Experience taught me what it means to have genuine faith, and I learned to not just believe in God but to know He is real and He is with me. I can see Him in everything and everyone I meet.

With an open mind and heart, I learned the importance of being aware of and holding tightly to the fact that God is the author of my story and has great plans for me if I am ready to receive them. It took some hard lessons for me to get to this point, but now I wake up each day ready to say, "This is the day the Lord has made; let me rejoice and be glad in it." If I begin the day with open arms of faith, even thanking Him for the unwanted situations which may not always be easy, it can free me from resentment. Life is broken up into twenty-four-hour segments for a reason. It is because He knows we can bear the weight of only one day at a time!

By living one day at a time, I am free from worrying about what is yet to come or getting stuck in the past. For I cannot rewrite history, nor can I predict the future if He is the author of my story and has already laid out my route with careful precision. That's not to say that I do not have free will. I get to make choices on a daily basis, and I am certainly a planner.

While I may not know the ultimate destination He has mapped out, I am still able to plan and chart a course for basic needs, schedules, and even long-term life goals. At the same time, I recognize life can throw curveballs and potholes can form in the road out of nowhere at any moment. We each have the freedom to make our own choices about what to do with our time, money, love, and, most especially, mental and emotional energies. If I spend that energy focusing too much on the past *or* the future, especially regarding events beyond my control, I will lose sight of enjoying God's gifts as they exist in the present.

I am blessed to wake up each day, place my trust in the Lord, and exhibit gratefulness for all that God has given me. Then, as each day ends, I get the opportunity to ask God to help me rest in Him and let His Spirit be my leading and driving force. Because of my relationship with Him and His loyalty to me through baptism, I can wake up to a new twenty-four-hour segment each day with forgiveness, and I know I will be supported by His strength as I go about my tasks. With gratitude, I am then ready to experience another beautiful day.

I have made it through the ups and downs set before me, continually growing in faith, because of what I've learned, the need to take things one day at a time, and the ability to live each day so fully and refreshed by God

While the foundation of my faith was laid at an early age through baptism and the truly remarkable example set by my parents, I continued to build upon and deepen my faith with each mile of my journey, painful as some of the stops along the road may have been. Each part of the trek has made me realize that my journey has been mapped out in a particular route all according to His plan even if I may have hoped for a GPS recalculation or rewiring of the brain at times.

The Mind Matters—Especially with Epilepsy

While I do have epilepsy, I make a point to avoid using the terminology, "I suffer from epilepsy." I actively choose not to refer to it as "suffering," instead turning my focus towards the many blessings in my life, especially those that have come as a result of my condition. I am extraordinarily grateful for the life I continue to live with epilepsy even though my route has had its challenges, sometimes even needing a U-turn and GPS recalibration, ever since being diagnosed back in 2006. I prefer to refer to "my condition" instead of "my suffering" because of how much these challenges have shaped my growth, both in spirituality and fortitude of character.

When you hear about suffering in connection to a medical condition, it typically implies the experience of pain and agony. If you look up the true definition of what suffering is, you might find that yes, it does imply pain, but at the same time, you'd also find one of the key synonyms for "to suffer" is "to endure."

I don't know about you, but when I consider the word "endure," or more specifically endurance, I visualize a runner. When someone runs a marathon, you call them a hero, a champion, someone who has remarkable stamina. On the other hand, you might call them crazy, but either way, you need not necessarily liken a runner to someone who is in pain—except for maybe after they finish the race. They are simply doing what must be done to come out as victors on the (crazy) marathon journey.

I have never personally run a marathon, nor am I enthusiastic about doing anything of the long-distance running nature. As my friends and family can attest, I will only ever run if someone is chasing me or if there is a fire. I will definitely run if I hit a home run and, of course, if the kids are in danger. Running around a track or without a destination just for fun, though, is out of the question. I have a vague understanding of the premise. I can certainly imagine, however, that in much the same way that a marathon is a test of endurance, my life with epilepsy is also a test of endurance, strength of will, and determination.

With all that in mind, I suppose it might be possible for me to train for, run, and even finish a marathon if I chose to put forth the dedicated effort. Surely, I'd have to walk half the time, if not more, though. Perhaps that is exactly how epilepsy, my own personal marathon, has unfolded. Sometimes I jog and sometimes I get carried (away in an ambulance, unfortunately), but for the most part, I keep enduring at a slow walk, step by step on a long, stretching road.

Just like the immeasurably wise group of sages from the 1990s, New Kids on the Block, once said, when life gets hard, things must be taken step by step. It is not always big steps, either. Sometimes we must take baby steps. These come in all shapes and sizes, too. For me, it was the baby steps of my miracle children. Then it was the baby steps of the twelve steps of recovery. Everything does happen for a reason, though, as the steps I learned in recovery turned out to be incredibly important for my mental health and self-discovery later in life. Perhaps most importantly, though, it was in recovery that I relied and built further upon the foundations of faith established in childhood, soon building my faith into a skyscraper of serenity and spirituality which was essential for being able to handle the biggest challenge of my life, the surgery to address my temporal lobe epilepsy.

While the saying might be trite, it is also remarkably true that every day is a gift. It has taken me some time, but I've finally come to thoroughly grasp this concept because, as cheesy as it might sound, every single day is a gift and that is why they call it the present. This daily marathon of living with epilepsy can, of course, be quite stressful and frightening. Like the shot that signals the start of a marathon, my marathon with epilepsy began with a bang when I had my first-ever seizure in 2006.

We have learned a lot about my specific type of seizures since then. Usually, when someone imagines an epileptic having a seizure, they envision the person shaking with convulsions, but that is only one aspect of a seizure. My episodes can happen in stages and over time, not all at once. Fortunately for me, they follow a pattern of the same or similar stages each time. Not every person with epilepsy will be this fortunate, however, as they may experience different symptoms in different ways or maybe not even experience the same sequence of events each time. This shaking portion is called the "clonic activity," and for me, this typically only happens after having had a pre-seizure warning, or what is called an aura.

For those unfamiliar, most epileptic seizures are preceded by this part of the process. This aura is, in fact, a focal onset seizure, sometimes referred to as a simple/partial seizure. It is during this phase of the seizure that a burst of electrical activity starts on one side of the brain and can cause several distinct symptoms. For me, I often experience a funny taste or smell, nausea, and sometimes even an awkwardly vivid sense of déjà vu.

These are usually very clear warning signs that a convulsive episode is soon to follow. If the focal seizure and abnormal electrical activity spreads to other parts of my brain, or generalizes, it will result in the sudden loss of consciousness or even a severe convulsive episode. Over the years, I have come to clearly recognize some of the many things that make my brain more susceptible to a seizure. For instance, sleep deprivation or too much caffeine are both significant triggers. And while some situations occasionally interrupt my sleep (the occasional emergency of a child's nightmare, for one), my sleep is in my control, as is the amount of caffeine I choose to consume, so these areas don't normally pose any threat to my epilepsy.

Thus, I try to control the things I can (something I learned a lot about through the serenity prayer, more on that later), and I stick to routine as much as possible. Getting up first thing in the morning, I say a quick prayer of, "Thank you for today, thank you for the opportunity to love, to give, and to be all that you need me to be." I make my bed. I exercise, not only because it is healthy as a now mid-forty-year-old woman who likes to indulge in a few sweet treats, but also because it is vital for my mind and my prayers (as you'll hear, I have found church can be just about anywhere you make it). It also wakes me up better than that small cup of coffee ever could. Well, that, and it's the only time I get to listen to the awesome rap and hard rock music from the '90s and 2000s that I wouldn't want my girls to be exposed to.

I try to eat at the usual times, and I take my medications at the same time every day. I am sure Jim might argue that I am particularly controlling about how things are stored in the refrigerator, but come on—who needs to put one piece of bacon in a 2-quart storage bin? That's just ridiculous overkill.

The element within my control and of the utmost value is my outlook and how I let it guide my decisions. Will I let challenges deter me or make me more determined? I have chosen to have the latter be my show of character.

I am not so strict with my routine that I get into a rut though I do sometimes have particular quirks that have become habits. For instance, always including certain songs in my playlist on certain days (Mondays just can't get started without Ludacris, Nate Dogg, Metallica, Incubus, Linkin Park and definitely my Backstreet Boys to round out the eclectic mix). I've developed other little quirks perhaps merely as a result of when my alarm goes off, of starting and ending times for the workout around the same time, and despite being committed to stopping at a certain time, I might see I've only gone 5.03 miles so I'll push it to 5.05 or from 5.999 just go that extra little bit to hit six even. But keeping that kind of rhythm makes me happy and excited to continue striving for good health overall since I can't always control those pesky epileptic neurons in my brain all of the time.

I certainly don't rigidly stick to military time as the cycle of routines could lead to a robotic life instead of living each day for the blessing it is. I try to remain aware being strict with my routines is ok, so long as I remember that each day is a brand-new opportunity to find beauty and meaning in all that I do. I try to remember that my future depends on what I do today. Even with the grand conductor knowing the ultimate path I will take and even when I don't know the destination ahead necessarily, I still have the freedom to make a choice to take the steps each day to make life better in every way, for both myself as well as for all those I encounter.

Learning to embrace and practice kindness towards myself and then spreading small (and hopefully, on occasion, big) acts of kindness to others each day pays incredible dividends. There is amazing beauty, meaning, and opportunity in each day for each of us. Being able to recognize this through all the troubles I have faced, and will continue to face, has been such a blessing, and I am so grateful that I have been able to fill my own story with joyful memories, laughter, and accomplishments in the face of adversity, good friends, and true happiness.

However, there are still other triggers for my seizures that we haven't pinpointed yet. I know that some of these triggers may be out of my control, which makes this condition so incredibly unpredictable on any given day. And lack of control and uncertainty is uncomfortable. Uncertainty that puts your health, your life, and your family in danger is downright terrifying and can feel paralyzing.

Once the initial shock of the first seizures wore off and I could finally wrap my not-so-normal brain around it, it took several years of living with the disease and its unpredictability to sink in and get used to, but the most important thing I learned to do was start to trust. I learned to trust my doctors and their advice for the best course of action for my treatment. I learned to trust myself and my body's cues for how to manage panic attacks, sleep, and seizure onset to prevent it from generalizing if possible. Most importantly, though, I learned to trust God and His angels above that my journey would continue being just that, a journey.

This journey is one with ups and downs. One with incredible highs and character-testing, challenging lows. Despite all that, though, I have learned to trust that my time on earth is far from over and that I have so much yet to live through. I can say that no matter what is thrown my way, each challenge that I have already risen to and conquered has been another tool from God's toolbox to strengthen me and prepare me for the next one that comes my way, even if it comes from out of the blue. It's like something I often say to Jim, *"The harder you fall, the higher you bounce!"* And how true that is. Each time I fall, I focus on how high I can get back up again to see all the amazing blessings around me. Like the episode in 2006. There were some hidden blessings in that horrific event. But we will come back to that a little later.

My experience on this marathon journey is an interesting one in that I do not see a traditional finish line nor do I think I'd want to. A finish line for me could be just that, finished. The end. *"Risa was a wonderful wife, mother, daughter. We will miss her. She was gone too soon."* Which is daunting, to say the least. I see no end markers with a buzzer, medals, or people there to cheer me on waving banners with my name. While I do have a great amount of support, especially from my incredible husband, my path can appear rather endless and quite unpredictable.

While walking this continuous road, I've not had any distinct odometer or "miles to go" signage, which has required me to nurture the faith upon which I was raised and trust the path as laid before me. In the words of Saint Jane de Chantal, *"We truly serve God when we walk without knowing the destination."* Such a beautiful and honest sentiment.

On that note of walking, though, the daily endurance test of simply walking with epilepsy has proven to be quite taxing and something that oftentimes requires a walking stick or the help of walking companions. For a person who likes to maintain unequivocal control of life, having seizures at random, inconvenient, and sometimes even perilous times is uncomfortable, to say the least. Life has felt like a constant state of God tapping me on the shoulder every so often to make sure I am reminded of who is in charge.

While the outcomes of each episode, nearly fatal car accidents and painful surgical procedures, were all favorable, they served as reminders that God is the one ultimately in control. I learned that no matter the outcome of my circumstances, He gave me this life and I can trust that He has carefully designed each step of my marathon.

For this reason, even when I don't know what twists, turns, mountains, or valleys may be ahead, I can trust that God has laid out this route for me exactly as He intended. I get the honor of serving Him by walking and enduring, despite not knowing the destination ahead. When I live each day showing my loved ones the same love that God has shown me, I am serving Him. Does that mean that I get it right every day? Not by any means.

I do not claim to be a life coach, nor do I live a perfect life. I know that I am perfectly imperfect, and my family will happily agree. As a wife, I still roll my eyes when the frustration of dirty dishes left out irritates me, especially just after having put the last clean ones away. As a mom, I struggle with little things that test my own temper and patience. I have my various good days and bad, sometimes finding myself needing to make apologies for causing hurt feelings to those around me because all this walking can be exhausting both mentally and physically.

Overall, though, despite the struggles and setbacks, I choose to allow my love and positivity to shine brighter and stronger than any little squalls in my life. Each day, my husband knows as he leaves for work that I love him with all my heart and just how eternally grateful I am for all he is doing to support and provide for our family. Every morning, when the girls wake up, I make sure to tell them how much I missed them while they were sleeping, and when they leave the house for school or other activities, I blow them a kiss that they always "catch." In return, they always blow one back to me, with me telling them, "*I'm keeping it!*" in reply.

I am grateful God has given me the strength to overcome the many difficult moments and allowed me to remain dedicated in my adoration of these amazing girls and in support of my loving husband. My hope is that they look at me not as suffering and not resentful of my troubles, but as an example of resilience. On a consistent basis, they see that I choose to keep on walking with faith that God is working in all of our lives, thus enabling me to stay focused on our blessings and all the hopeful things to come. This all-encompassing, daily choice and deep faith overshadow whatever fears may arise from unexpected challenges, those difficult moments, and the weight of any worries that come my way.

The phrase that I hope my children will most remember me by is what I've always told them, *"God loves you. Mommy loves you. And there is nothing in this world that you could do to ever make me stop loving you."* It is what my parents always told me and it has always made me feel safe, loved, protected, and forgiven.

That is the unconditional love that every child should feel from their parents. It is the security I was blessed to have and am now able to pass along to my own. They should have security in their heart and mind that there is nothing in the world they could do or be that could ever make me give up on them or cause me to stop loving them. We all make mistakes, and these girls have witnessed firsthand that I too need to make apologies sometimes. Giving and accepting apologies is part of real life, but no mistake would ever be too big to halt this mama's love.

I remind them that God created their hearts, and I carried those heartbeats inside my own body before bringing them into the light of this world. It is because of this mother-daughter connection that when they hurt, I hurt. So, hopefully, when I love them, demonstrate faith, and keep them positive, they feel it too, as they are truly a part of my own heartbeat walking around outside of my own body.

When they are grown and my time on this earth is done, they will still know my silly mom-isms. I eagerly look forward to being blessed to see my girls celebrate graduations, weddings, and, should the day come that God chooses to bless me with enough time to see my girls make me a grandmother, I will absolutely be whispering the love and truth that "*I love you to the moon and back*" to that beautiful next generation. Sometimes the mommy mantras of positivity get me an eye roll, but I have learned to be okay with that because no matter how people view my positivity, it is what carries me through even the most difficult days.

"*Chin up, buttercup! It's never too late to turn the day around!*" "*Every coin has two sides—unless you're a magician trying to cheat, but hey, either way...it's time to flip the coin and look on the bright side!*" One of my personal favorites even in the worst of crises, "*Don't freak out, we'll figure it out!*" While they may be a little cheesy, I usually do get a smile along with an occasional eye roll.

It is because of this chosen attitude of positivity and gratitude that I try to set the example for my girls. They see that even Mom, despite all her challenges and struggles, chooses to focus on the rainbow and not the scary storm. They learn to see the world through a lens of blessing instead of burden. They see that since I can do these things regardless of my circumstances, they too can tackle stress and struggle head-on with the same blessings-outweigh-burden and faith-over-fear mentality.

Every day it is love, faith, my family and positivity that keeps me going...and coffee, of course. I know the love coming from God is what keeps me here on earth, along with a host of personal angels who have been actively watching over me. While it may sound like I have a 100% positive, love-and-light mentality *all* the time, I have experienced the gamut of emotions along my marathon. I've been tired (*When is this going to end?*), frustrated (*Why me? Why again?*), angry, and afraid too. Emotions that are all normal for such a long journey, especially after having had the seizures continue after a supposedly "curative" procedure.

While these feelings of negativity are normal and expected while managing this disease, keeping any of them bottled up is dangerous. Keeping fear bottled up is like endlessly filling a balloon and expecting it never to pop. It's normal if it does pop, of course, but fear tends to manifest itself in other damaging behaviors, for me at least. I tend to become short-tempered, withdrawn, and bitter towards the loved ones who need me the most, causing them frustration and discouragement as a result. What's more, if I'm keeping the fears bottled up, they aren't mind readers and are unable to understand why I am acting poorly towards them.

In the same way, anger is a dangerously contagious emotion. When you let anger pop, it tends to explode, infuriating or causing hurt and pain to those around you, and likely lending itself to a domino effect and cycle of more anger and pain. And when one domino falls, everyone falls, making it that much more difficult to get back up and keep momentum moving forward in a positive manner.

When I step back and reflect upon my situation and my life, having this type of epilepsy isn't all that bad. It could be so much worse. I have amazing doctors and medical coverage. I have the gift of my family; I have a beautiful home with food and warmth. Even on those coldest of snowy days in Upstate New York, we were able to find the blessings within our cozy, warm house, like hot cocoa and snuggling under blankets to watch movies together. On the unbearably hot days when the air conditioner seemed to not want to work, we still had plenty of sunscreen to prevent burns. We could find relief with a cool swim in the ocean or shade under an umbrella and enjoy the beauty of God's creation outdoors instead of just complaining about all of the heat. Especially since we were begging for warmth under ten feet of snow just months prior!

Most things in life come down which perspective you choose to adopt. As the old adage goes, is the glass half full or half empty? I've found that when I look at things as half full, I can get through just about anything with greater confidence and the bolstered fortitude to keep moving forward on the path, the marathon. Heck, if I thought about the marathon only being halfway finished, I would be fixated on how much farther I needed to go and how exhausted it's already been! But if I think about how far I've already walked and the interesting things I've seen and all that I've accomplished, I'm much more motivated to keep on truckin'.

I've endured some painfully difficult times to reach these realizations, but it indeed is true, your perspective can give you wings or weigh you down. It can become your prison, or it will become your passport. When you have been to the depths of the darkest valley or climbed the highest, most difficult peaks, your perspective about everything around you is transformed. The little things that used to be such nuisances are just that—little things. They become insignificant in the grand scheme. Challenges that used to seem overwhelmingly strenuous and stressful are an easy hike compared to the mountain you once conquered. That 5K I might never have considered in the past might actually look feasible. If I were to ever consider truly running.

And when things become too heavy to bear, and the fear creeps in, threatening to paralyze you—you take things one second at a time...one hour at a time...one day at a time, because as my wise mother always said, "This too shall pass." I have faith with each milestone and mile marker that my journey is far from over, that my finish line is far down the road many happy, blessed days from now. I chose faith over fear in my life, and I will keep living each glorious moment of the marathon. I probably won't be running, though.

Loss, Love, and Learning to Listen

During my freshman year of school, my parents sold the house in New Jersey and moved to Philadelphia, which made it very easy to get away from the stresses of an Ivy League environment for mental breaks every once in a while. Throughout college, like many of my Catholic counterparts at that age, I wasn't *as* good about going to church every Sunday, but faith was still a constant.

Despite the stressors of going to an intense Ivy League school, I found myself traveling the short distance home quite a bit. I even found a great deal of in attending church in those times and praying for strength to get through the week and praising for relief on weekends. It was nice to feel like attending church was my choice as an adult, instead of the all-too-familiar feeling of being dragged with my parents as a kid.

Although we were more spread out during college, my high school friends and I tried to gather during winter and summer breaks. Some time together was better than none, so while those gatherings were few and far between, we cherished them. We determined that some time together and enjoying each other was better than none, so while those gatherings were few and far between, they were cherished and worth it.

Unfortunately, both of my grandmothers became ill during my college years. I was very close to both of them. They were so strong in their faith, and they passed along to me that same sense of faith and showed me how they really trusted in God's plan for them. They had such faith to go through sometimes awful circumstances, and that faith continued to carry them through to enter His heavenly kingdom. Their wisdom and advice have stayed with me all these years, and I get to experience the joy of being able to remember those wonderful nuggets of wisdom from time to time.

What's even more awesome is that I continue to pass down to my children one of my Babci's best sayings, which was, "If you pray, why worry—and if you worry, why pray?" In fact, why even worry? When I worry, I only end up suffering more by getting stuck repeatedly in the "what ifs" of the future. If I let "what ifs" be positive and prayerful, rather than the worst possible outcome, I am better able to stay present with my loved ones and better able to practice gratitude and enjoy each experience without having to worry about problem-solving until the actual problem arises.

After all, it has taken some hard lessons, but I have come to understand that being grateful is entirely different than practicing gratitude. When you think of being grateful, you may be alluding to just another way of saying you are "thankful" for something, as in "I am so grateful for your help." For me, being grateful and having gratitude are wholly different. I have come to understand that gratitude is a daily mindset that takes practice and requires that I extend my love outwards, shining light and positivity on those around me. Saying "thank you" is an obvious way for everyday common politeness, but I have always tried to go above and beyond to recognize that you never know what someone may be going through.

It's the little things that add up. I recognized during the pandemic that the grocery store workers were just as much frontline workers as those in the hospital because everyone needs to buy food! When I would do my shopping during that pandemic, it was amazing to see how touched those workers were to hear me say, "Thank you for being here so that I can feed my family." When I had my driver's license suspended and couldn't get my groceries (or do back-to-school shopping), I relied on so many delivery services. You'd be surprised how many of those drivers are stunned to be asked, "Do you need anything? I know you've been on the road for a while. Can I offer you water?" Those little kindnesses are hopefully things that can then be passed along to others in the world.

I have also noticed that my girls now follow in my footsteps of being a little less self-centered. Spreading love and light doesn't have to be complex. It can be as simple as listening. It was once brought to my attention that LISTEN and SILENT are made up of the same letters. Just listening is an act of kindness and a way to offer my full and undivided presence, and so is listening after asking, "How are you?" and meaning it. When you say, "I'll keep you in my prayers" to someone who is going through a hard time, it is important that you really do mean it and, more importantly, that you follow through with that offer. That kindness will mean the world to them.

My mom's mom (Mom Mom), probably the most tolerant or perhaps driven to be the craziest (in a fun way) of all the Maries, mostly due to the six children she gave birth to, was diagnosed with pancreatic cancer during my junior year of college. Throughout that awful battle, though, she did her best to put her pain aside to always show all her thirteen grandchildren love. She always found ways to make us laugh despite her pain, and we saw that it was possible to be strong and face difficulty and pain with peace and strength.

The way she so gracefully handled her medical challenges right up until her death could be summed up by the words of St. Francis of Assisi, "Make me an instrument of thy peace. Where there is hatred, let me sow love, where there is injury, pardon; where there is doubt, faith; where there is despair, hope; where there is darkness, light; and where there is sadness, joy." She refused to let us see just how much pain she was in and kept all those around her laughing throughout her fight because it was important to her that she be a source of joy to others, regardless of her own circumstances.

When she was nearing the end of her battle in the final stages of cancer, she was in hospice care, and she continued, even then, to put on a brave face. If you had asked me or any of my family, we would have never known she was intentionally under-medicating herself so that she could still maintain her mental acuity to be present and enjoy her time with us. She often exuded the delight of dripping sarcasm as she greeted those visiting her or the caretakers who would often be nearby. She even went so far as to "fire" some of the staff.

She regularly had us laughing, and she would often embrace us with her love and warmth up until her final moments. While I didn't know it at the time, having a role model like her (someone who could stay positive in the face of such pain and have the faith to grind through that pain) would soon become the strength I needed to tap deep into when I would need it the most in my own life to deal with my own pain and struggles.

Last Minute Date to Last a Lifetime

It is only mildly surprising in retrospect that Jim and I wound up together, yet it still would never have been something we could have predicted. We first met all the way back in seventh grade when my mom taught our confirmation religious education class. We were both raised Catholic, sharing common values from the start of our friendship, but a romantic connection just wasn't something that ever crossed our minds.

Our story is such an interesting and amusing one, too. We were always just good buddies, maybe even like siblings. We were so close through middle and high school. We both lived in such a small district that we even shared a couple of the same classes, including a foreign language class. We would see each other and our families at social, school, and church events regularly.

Jim ran track while I played softball. We both had older siblings and a solid group of fun and goofy friendships. It was not an era yet for social media cyberbullying back then, but "real" bullying existed, and our circle of friends all stood up for each other. Our group of friends liked spending time together and hanging out in whatever free time we had.

My best friend Theresa was the one I spent the most time with. I met her before Jim, on the bus in fifth grade. Our houses were in separate developments, but I could see the back of her house from my backyard when the trees were bare. As with any friendship, though, as both Theresa and I got older, we each became busy with all the normal extracurriculars of life. She became caught up with her various dance lessons, and I focused a lot of my time on varsity softball and a rigorous academic schedule.

We found time on the weekends for sleepovers with friends and talked about boys. I mean I thought I had found my soulmate at eight years old in the incomparable Jordan Knight. Then thought I had found true love at first sight at 16 and despite my damaged brain I remember my heart feeling like it was fluttering 311 beats per minute! Back then though, Jim was always just one of the guys we hung out with – never viewed by either of us in a romantic sense. I had my share of dates and boyfriends during high school, some from our school, some who graduated years prior, and some from other schools altogether. I experienced breakups, heartache, and made some irresistible but fated mistakes. Some first loves that caused me pain, made me insane, and love whose impact remains. But that's what made the road to Jim that much more winding and remarkable. The others who broke my heart were pointing me on my way and preparing me for my life with Jim as devastating as it all may have seemed at the time.

Theresa started to date one of our classmates, Bill, during senior year of high school, and they ended up sticking to the relationship all through college, even when she went to school in North Carolina and he in New Jersey. Our core group of friends spread out to various schools along the Eastern Seaboard, including Jim who started studying pre-med and played in the marching band at Penn State University.

It was through lots of long hard nights studying and balancing a *lot* of extracurriculars (not to mention that I am awesome at taking tests) that I was able to get into and attend the University of Pennsylvania Wharton Undergraduate School of Business in Philadelphia. My college years were filled with hard work, amazing friendships, and, unfortunately establishing the groundwork for some bad habits that had been rooted in some deep-seated insecurities. More on all of that later.

Having gone our separate ways after high school but still sporadically in touch throughout college, the idea that Jim and I might one day date each other was still entirely ridiculous to me. That is, until one fateful afternoon in January of 2004.

Just before our roads so fatefully intersected, though, I had finally done it. After all the long hours and hard work studying for my undergraduate degree at Wharton, I earned my bachelor's degree in marketing and management from Penn in the spring of 2003! After that amazing accomplishment, I began working for one of the pharmaceutical divisions at Johnson & Johnson in Sales Analytics.

Theresa and I would still get together whenever we could find the time, and the commute from Philadelphia to New Jersey was pretty manageable. That I-95 corridor could be quite a bear if you didn't time it right. But, with good planning, it was smooth sailing. Fortunately for me, too, I was able to work out an earlier shift with my manager (7:15 a.m.–4 p.m.) to be able to beat both ends of rush hour traffic.

As I reflect on that, it must be the likely beginnings of my early-bird lifestyle taking shape. I did, after all, have to be up by 6 a.m. to hit the road in time to get to my desk no later than 7:15 a.m. In my department, there was another recent grad as well. She had moved to Philadelphia from out of state and we both ended up in the same Leadership Development Program. As it turned out, she also moved into an apartment not too far from my parents' house in Philadelphia, and so we shared a similar commute, though she wasn't quite as much of an early riser as I was, and her manager wasn't as forgiving with her schedule as mine.

As we began to socialize outside of work on the weekends, I was able to introduce her to some of my local friends, and she even joined us at the beach for some fun weekends. As time went on, she made more friends and would occasionally invite me to her social gatherings as well. In the late fall of 2003, I got a wedding invitation for one of the girls that Theresa and I had gone to school with back in high school.

As luck would have it, my co-worker had recently introduced me to a guy, and we had started a casual dating relationship. The timing was perfect because this meant I wouldn't have to find a date or go to the wedding all by myself. Our carefully crafted journey and God's intentions for the life Jim and I were destined to live were about to be revealed. Thank God for the broken road indeed! Turns out the guy I was casually dating and counting on to be my plus-one to the wedding wasn't into me after all. He dumped me days before the wedding, and I was left high and dry.

Of course, being that I was at a loss for what to do, I called Theresa lamenting my minor heartbreak. The guy was kind of a bore so, in the end, his loss ended up definitely becoming my gain! Regardless of how lame the guy might have been, being rejected is never fun and still carried a bit of a sting. What irritated me the most, though, was the fact that now I had to find someone at the last minute to go with me to the wedding.

Theresa, in all her wild and fantastic glory, simply said, "Call Jimmy! He's living with his parents—studying for med school, he'll totally go!" I told her there was no way I could call Jim; it would sound too desperate. I hadn't talked to him in like a year, anyway, and it would just be so weird to call him for this.

So, Theresa got even more bold and said, "Fine, I'll call him for you!" And that is exactly what she did! I couldn't believe it. So, at that moment, Theresa, who was still with her high school boyfriend (and now husband), called Jim on my behalf, seeing as I was feeling so sour and not ready for more rejection, having just been dumped.

Theresa made this fateful phone call and has since filled in all the blanks that I missed in that initial phone conversation. He picked up the phone and Theresa just jumped right in with her fantastic schemes. "Hey Jim, will you go to Kristen's wedding with me on Saturday?" Kind, but clearly confused, Jim said "Sure, but what about your boyfriend?" She giggled, "Oh, he's going with Risa."

To this day, his response is absolutely hilarious and one of the main reasons we have been married all these years. He said, "Okay, but why can't I go with Marisa?" (And *that* sentence is the reason we are married today.) Theresa quickly responded with, "Perfect, she'll pick you up at 3," and then called me and cheered, "Of course he'll go with you, dummy!"

I can clearly remember nervously driving up to Jim's house and feeling a little awkward as I parked at the end of the driveway. I did what any respectable person does, and I called him to let him know that I'd arrived, and then I saw the garage door open. It had been a couple of years since I had seen him in person, and I wasn't sure what to expect.

Then, as the garage door lifted, he ducked his head under and came out dressed in his suit pants and a red shirt to match his strawberry-red hair. He had been using the time of living with his parents and studying for med school to also work as a lifeguard, tutor, and apparently lift some weights because this Jim had some serious muscles that I didn't remember seeing before!

As he continued to strut out of the garage and towards me with his sunglasses on, he suavely flung his suit jacket over his shoulder. All the while, I'm sitting there thinking to myself, *Oh my goodness! What happened to Jim (in a good way, of course)!?! I have got to find my perfume and fast!!* My heart was feverishly racing! Then other thoughts caught me off guard. *What if too much time has passed since we saw each other? Was this going to be an awkward time together?"* Jim was looking capital F.I.N.E., and I was feeling...something...was it nerves?

Whatever those feelings were, Jim got in the car, easy breezy, and it was as if no time had passed between us at all. We had a blast at that wedding—we laughed, we flirted, we danced—we had so much fun that we ended up going to three more weddings that year, and we even took a trip to Scotland for New Year's to see how well we could tolerate each other as traveling companions! Things went so well for us that by the following year, August of 2005, to be exact, he asked me to be his wedding date for life! Thus, wedding planning for the following fall began to take place.

We may have taken the circuitous or scenic route to find each other for life, but our wedding song captures it perfectly—because God did, indeed, "Bless the Broken Road," and He continues to bless the ups and downs, the hills and mountains we have climbed. Jim has proven time and again that he is my absolute *rock*. We have brought two amazing children into this world, and with his background in medicine, we have been so much better equipped to handle the challenges of this wonderful disease of mine. It hasn't all been easy, though, and we would soon come to find out that the broken road would continue to have cracks and need repaving all along the way.

Seized the (Wedding) Day

My first seizure happened two months before Jim and I got married. It would be one of the first of many bumps along our blessed but broken road.

I awoke in a fog. My mind was heavy and confused, and I was most definitely uncomfortable. This wasn't my bed. There was beeping all around me from machines, and I thought to myself, *Where am I, and whose alarm is going off?* The number of machines connected to my head and body was quite disturbing. Despite the fuzziness of my mind, it was clear that I was in the emergency room. The scariest part of the whole thing, though, was that I had absolutely zero recollection of how or why I got there.

It was at this point that Jim informed me that I had suffered a grand mal seizure the night before. Wait, hold on a second. *A what?* Surely, this was a nightmare. I couldn't imagine that this was my real life. This couldn't be happening—this was a nightmare. I thought for a brief second that maybe it was just a bad migraine since I got those regularly as a teenager and I had even gotten several in the months leading up to this particular incident. I was working long and stressful hours as a data analyst, too. Maybe I was just stretched too thin, and the hours were getting to me.

I mean, no, they were not as crazy as, say, Wall Street hours that a lot of my fellow Wharton counterparts were putting in, but they were long hours of sitting and staring at a computer and, well, computing. *All of that on top of the extra stress of planning my wedding just two months away, it must just be a bad migraine, right? Yeah, that's got to be all this is. I'm sure as soon as the wedding passes and life gets back to normal, I'll be totally fine. But my goodness, thank God that Jim knew what to do (see, divine appointments, right?)!* I had never had a seizure before, and of course, Jim would be there for the first one and would know exactly what to do (med school, remember!) in that situation.

To this day, though, with all the dozens of MRIs and invasive testing I have undergone, we have yet to discover or understand the exact cause or genesis of my epilepsy.

At the time of that first episode, we really had no idea what was going on, and the initial MRIs showed abnormal activity in my right frontal lobe, but a diagnosis wouldn't come until later. The doctors asked if I had ever had febrile seizures or meningitis as a child or if I had experienced some sort of trauma at birth. None of those applied, so we considered this 2006 episode as a one-off, rare occurrence. It was definitely alarming, but it didn't give us reason (yet) for long-term concern. It was more baffling than anything. Instead of worrying, though, we had bigger things to focus on.

Pushing the stress of the one seizure and weird little blip aside, all that was left to do was tie the knot, have two become one and all that jazz, and have life get back to normal! Action plan initiated. It was a little daunting to think about getting married just two months after such a significant event, but we were so close to the big day, and if I hadn't already known that I was meant to be with Jimmy before, I for sure knew I was going to be in good hands with a medical professional should anymore "blips" happen!

I just needed to keep breathing, keep remembering to take care of myself a little better and stay calm. Thank God for Jimmy. Thank God he wasn't freaked out either—I guess it was a little late to back out now, anyway! We had already come this far. Here we go...

The time for the wedding had finally arrived. And what a marvelous event it was. We were blessed to enter into the holy sacrament of marriage and celebrate in front of friends and family as we vowed to love, honor, cherish, and laugh at each other's jokes in good times and in bad times. As it turns out, those words at the altar would come to mean so very much because of the "bad times" and bumps in the road of our marriage. And those bad times, well, they were unfortunately not just associated with my epilepsy, as life would soon reveal.

Leading up to the "big day" my parents always made it a point to remind me that it is not the wedding, but the marriage that matters most. A wedding is just a single day, a one-time celebration. Important as it may be, the focus is not that of the celebration on that day but rather the vows you share, the promises you make, and most importantly the life that you build together. Focusing on these vows and these promises as you build your life together is what really sets the stage for a healthy marriage.

Healthy marriages are something both Jim and I have seen firsthand in the remarkable examples set by our parents whose marriages have incredibly stood the test of time. From the time they made the commitment at the altar, they stayed true to their own vows and weathered the good and the bad, in sickness and in health. In a world that would just as soon see a marriage fall apart as it would see it last, it is such a gift to have role models who valued marriage and demonstrated that it is possible to navigate all the twists and turns that life can bring. It is because of their example that we knew the substantial commitment involved in a marriage. Because of our parents, we knew a marriage entailed more than just saying "I do" at the altar. Entering into the holy sacrament of marriage meant valuing true faithfulness and showing continuous support. It meant being a team, practicing patience, communicating constructively, having fun, and finding forgiveness.

To see our own parents work as partners really shaped how Jim and I entered into our own union, knowing what the commitment meant and what it would take for our own partnership to succeed just the same. They taught us that no marriage is perfect and that you must work at it (though it isn't always hard work when you love your spouse like a best friend). You must keep your marriage well cared for just like you would a garden...with love and constant attention never to be taken for granted. The exchange of vows, the seeds that had been planted so many years before with an easy friendship had truly blossomed, and we felt so very grateful and hopeful as we looked forward to spending the rest of our lives together.

After all the excitement of the wedding had finally quieted down, things seemed to stay in that sense of quiet for a while. In fact, things were quiet, and we enjoyed our life as the new Mr. and Mrs. James Scott for all of 2007. Little did we know that that was just the calm of the eye of the storm. With Jim having gone to med school in Long Island while I was living and working in Pennsylvania and having done the long-distance thing, we were both hoping he'd get matched to a local residency program.

When the time finally came to be able to check the status of where he'd been matched, I was the one who had to log into the website and check because he was, you guessed it, busy at the hospital. I remember being so nervous just opening the internet to check and see his results. It felt like I was a kid again, checking my SAT scores or opening a letter from a college where I'd applied.

The nerves had me shaking in my boots (or was that the epilepsy?). As our path revealed itself so clearly and intentionally, Jim got matched to a program at UMDNJ in South Jersey and, of course, they had an unfathomably rigorous residency program he had to attend while I was entrenched in the enjoyably and intellectually stimulating work of data coordination and management with my own colleagues. Queue anxiety, excitement, dread, and every other emotion possible.

Prior to his match, we had what felt like (to us, at least) a luxurious two-bedroom apartment in South Plainfield, NJ, and we had settled into a fantastic routine as newlyweds. It seemed like genuine wedded bliss together. We kept renting the apartment, too afraid to set roots down anywhere until we knew for sure where we would end up with Jim's program. But with the lease finally up in South Plainfield during 2008 just before Jim got his match results, my parents lovingly offered to provide free boarding until we could figure out our next steps.

The uncertainty of not knowing when or where to set down roots prior to Jim's match felt a bit overwhelming, especially for a couple of newlyweds. We were still simply choosing to be encouraged and to look at the bright side of things...of course, that all became somewhat more difficult throughout 2008 when we realized the episode of 2006 wasn't a blip. My brain went haywire. I began having more episodes and had to be hospitalized four times within the year, even suffering some extremely serious post-seizure delusions in the process. At least this is also when I got some official answers to what in the world was going on with me...

Diagnosed, Discouraged, but Not Defeated

It was in 2008, after several more MRIs, that I was officially diagnosed with Right Frontal Mesial Temporal Lobe Epilepsy. This meant that I had an abnormality seen on the MRI within the medial or internal structures of the right temporal lobe. To this day, though, with all the dozens of MRIs and invasive testing that I have undergone, we have yet to discover or understand the exact cause or genesis of my epilepsy. Though I suffered from migraines as a teenager after a head injury, the doctors have consistently concluded that the two are not at all related.

Seizures often begin in a structure of the brain called the hippocampus or surrounding area. This section of the brain is responsible for a great deal of memory storage and retrieval. The right temporal lobe also plays a part in spatial memory, which might be the reason why I can't remember where I put my keys half of the time or remember how to get anywhere without a map, even if I've been there a hundred times. Many doctors have inquired as to whether I ever suffered febrile seizures or meningitis as a child or if I experienced some sort of trauma at birth. They've asked about head trauma as well.

Even though I did, in fact, suffer a head injury from falling off a wave runner when I was thirteen years old, the doctors assured me that the lesion they saw on my brain was far too deep to have been caused by that accident.

There is a scar or lesion on my right frontal temporal lobe, the part of the brain associated with learning and remembering non-verbal information, storing and retrieving memories...all things I still struggle with to this day. Fortunately (or unfortunately, depending on how you look at it), I can still remember hearing the news and the doctors telling me those awful words, "You have a lesion on your brain. We could do surgery to remove it." It felt so matter of fact and direct—no empathy, just words.

Jim and I both nixed that idea at the time because we felt as if this was far too drastic a measure, seeing as I had only had just a few seizures in my life. I mean, they wanted to take out part of my brain! That sounded absolutely insane. Like something out of a science fiction horror movie or something. But things still didn't feel quite steady for me, even when I started taking the medications they prescribed. Jim and I eventually moved in with my parents in Philly so that I didn't have to be alone as much and, as a bonus, we could start saving for our own house.

Back to the series of events that led to this whole big ordeal. It all started out as several back-to-back migraines at the beginning of the year 2008. Looking back now, we should have realized that these were warning signs of what was to come. Despite being somewhat unaware that these were warning signs, my brain decided to finally surrender to its own faultiness, and I ended up having another in what would become a series of grand mal seizures, this time in the middle of the night, and I ended up hospitalized in late February, which resulted in an extended stay in the critical care unit.

When I was finally able to return to our apartment, I had four anti-seizure medications and still no clear answers about what was wrong with my head. This is when the doctors came back and informed me that the report was showing that I had a lesion on my right frontal temporal lobe and that was when I was officially diagnosed with Temporal Lobe Epilepsy in March of 2008. To say that the official diagnosis ended up being both a blessing and a curse is a huge understatement. It was nice to finally know exactly what it was that caused my brain to go haywire, but at the same time, it left me with a devastating sense of sadness and wasn't easy to fully accept.

It has been said, "Knowing is half the battle," but I am not sure that this is true. Even though I finally knew what was wrong, it felt like there was so much more than half a battle left to fight. Sure, I was grateful to learn what the issue was. But there was so much more that needed to happen, so much work needed to be done, so much more of this journey yet to be traveled. Although I had been dealing with some of the disease for a while, being given the diagnosis and having a fuller understanding of what the ultimate issue was provided a brand-new ballgame. So, for me, knowing was just the first inning.

One thing I will say about 2008, even though it was a giant buzzkill on the health front, I still had other things to keep me cheering. Being an avid Phillies fan, I can honestly say that the only redeeming quality about that ridiculous year was having a World Series victory for my beloved and clearly awesome team! Other than that, though, it was a downright awful year, and I wouldn't even get to see my World Series Champs in the parade down Broad Street. Talk about a bummer! This is, however, when I would start down the path of perspective. At least I got to see the games. I wasn't blind. I was still alive and coherent enough to enjoy watching my favorite Fightin' Phillies team.

Looking back now, it is easy to see how clever God can be. In this case, it seems that it worked out well that we had moved in with my folks because my mom really enjoyed having the company since my dad commuted to Boston for work during the week. Though, I will say, I'm not sure she also enjoyed the company of our two cats, but she was kind enough to tolerate them. I absolutely loved being back in Society Hill, and the fact that I got to spend quality time with my mom again, that is something I will always cherish. Time, as I have learned through the years, is something that I will always treasure.

It seems that 2008 was a year that held a lot of new experiences for me. It was in 2008 that I had to surrender my driver's license to the medical review board because of my seizures. While it may have been only temporary, it felt like a significant deal. Because of the epilepsy diagnosis, I had my driving privileges removed for an extended period of time. This is when I was forced to put on my Girl Scout and business planning creativity pants to learn how to make work...work. It was a steep lesson in learning to be entirely okay (and not shy!) asking for help. I'd gotten good at asking God for help, but in this season, I also had to learn how to ask other people for help, and it was definitely a humbling experience.

Moving to the city also worked out well because it made getting around with a license much easier. I could get almost everywhere I needed to be by public transit, and everything else I needed could usually be reached within walking distance. If we had been living in almost any other place, this likely would not have been possible, and I would have needed to tap deep into my creativity skills. And I did have to get creative from time to time, but for the most part, while the whole situation was not ideal, there were so many amazing positive aspects that turned out to be real blessings for me.

Brain Glitches and Priority Switches

Taking a minute to zip forward to June of 2008 now, and those warning migraines began to return. I remember spending a weekend in late June with a truly horrific two-day combo of migraines that turned into one mighty and nasty seizure, and that resulted in me having to be carried out on a hospital stretcher. Getting to know the local ER staff was not my idea of how to spend my summer vacation, but I did that anyway. I spent some time at the hospital, and then ended up for the rest of the weekend on the couch...but at least the couch was a nice and comfy one...it's the little things that helped.

The hospital staff were kind enough to let me out to go home within a week this time, a bonus in and of itself, as anyone who has spent time in the hospital knows. Let's face it, the less time in the hospital, the better. I enjoy spending time in the hospital about as much as I do at a Phillies versus Mets game at Shea Stadium when the Mets are winning. There was no indication as to what prompted the event this time, though, which was discouraging. I was taking all my meds, and I was avoiding all the things that we thought might have been triggers at the time. It just seemed to come out of nowhere this time, and it was so unclear and uncertain that it was really scary.

At this time, I was still working...or attempting to, at least...in hopes that staying busy would get my mind off, well, my mind. But by the time July came around, Jim and I had prayerfully decided that the day-to-day uncertainty was enough for me to part ways with my day job, and so I put in my two-weeks' notice.

It was a difficult decision but also a decision that was really a no-brainer for the sake of my brain (you're welcome, pun absolutely intended). It was the beginning of many similar decisions I would have to make while handling the complexities of living with epilepsy. There were moments, and still are, frankly, where I can't help but feel like the Scarecrow from Oz, wishing things could be better, if I only had a brain, after all. I often felt like there were decisions that most people would have no issues making, but for me, everything just seemed to have an added weight that I didn't know how to lift, and that caused a lot of problems. As I'd soon find out, I was going to end up making decisions that would cause real strife in my health, my marriage, and my family.

Each of these decisions, both good and bad, were ones that I suppose I had to make to be exposed to the opportunity to learn valuable lessons that would eventually lead me to growth spurts of faith. These lessons were also a means for gaining valuable tools enabling us to better manage the unpredictability and stress that comes with such a complicated disease as epilepsy, and I am so grateful for each of them. When I decided to leave my job, I learned one of the first important lessons: prioritization. With everything that was going on, it just seemed to make sense that I would set aside my work and spend more time focusing on making sure we knew how to best cope with the weight of epilepsy, which can be quite heavy from time to time.

So, when Jim and I finally decided that leaving work was the right thing for me to do, it was not an easy decision to make. I enjoyed my job and loved the community of friends I had built with my co-workers. They were great people, and I very much enjoyed the time I was able to spend with them on a weekly basis. But this was a necessary decision for the sake of the health of my brain. It was a decision that came with a great deal of fear that people would look at me and think that I was just wasting my Wharton degree, a fear that would not relent for years to come.

I also suffered from the fear that my epilepsy would leave me adrift, hexed with complications and aimless in this world. I had such a purpose and drive with my job. Giving that up felt like giving up the purpose I thought I had. I prayed endlessly for seizure freedom. It was a very discouraging time, but I can't help but recall famous words from an old dead Greek philosopher, Epicurus. He said, "You don't develop courage by being happy in your relationships every day. You develop it by surviving difficult times and challenging adversity," or in other words, you must push through the challenges to become courageous, and so I did. I left my job, and I prayed for purpose in those days and weeks and months that followed. I thank God that I did, too, because 2008 continued to go downhill, and life would have had greater issues if I was still trying to work as well.

It was discouraging to me that it seemed no matter how diligent I was about taking all my medications, I continued to have seizures. I had another one in September and then a particularly scary incident at the end of October. Thankfully, I was at home, but it was yet another trip to the emergency room, where I ended up having three more. Even after the convulsions had stopped, I began suffering from post-seizure delusions and I even threatened the security guards. Evidently, it was so bad that I told one of the biggest guards, "Don't take another step towards me, THUNDOR!" and when the doctor asked if she could take my pulse, I said, "You wanna take my pulse? Fine, take it!" and I threw my Gatorade bottle at him.

They found that it was probably necessary to keep me sedated for the time being. It was more than a little unnerving to awaken...in the hospital...in restraints. This is when they had to adjust my medication yet again. It put everyone on edge as we were still trying to find the right medication dosages and find which ones were working. But one thing became crystal clear in those moments at the hospital: this lesion was the ultimate cause of all this wild behavior. Still, we didn't know how or why it got there, what might trigger my next seizure, or why certain medications weren't working.

A New Hope (Eat Your Heart Out, Luke Skywalker)

I began feeling like something of a doomed science experiment. Like I was hexed I was some sort of human lab rat. It was awful and terrifying. It's like the doctors were just constantly throwing the dice at me and seeing if they could get a couple of sevens...and if that didn't work, see ya, head on back to the ER, thanks for playing! Thankfully, though, after the final medication adjustment of 2008, we found what felt like pretty solid footing and said our prayers that 2009 would bring about a better year of peace, comfort, joy, and excitement. We had complete faith that after the craziness of the prior year, 2009 was going to be a better year with wonderful new beginnings. And oh boy (or girl, I should say), did 2009 really deliver!

There were certainly a few moments in the beginning of 2009 when things felt like they were going so well that I was starting to get, dare I even say it, bored! I would look back at this time and learn to be grateful for that season of calm before the storm. Jim and I decided that because things were feeling solid enough on the health front, it would make sense (not to mention *cents*, because we had saved enough for that house we were saving for) for me to go back to work. I was so thrilled to find a job in the Wharton MBA Program Office—talk about full circle. I could easily take the bus from Society Hill to University City, and they all understood my condition and accommodated the occasional need for flexible hours when necessary. The job was lower stress, I made great friends in the office, and it was heartwarmingly nostalgic to be back on campus. During that time, when I was on campus and revisiting old memories, I kept in touch with my friends from that memorable senior year via email. We would all send weekly updates that we called our High/Low update. Our emails have since become more monthly because life can get quite hectic as families expand and responsibilities mount, but they are cherished nonetheless.

    I had a lot of hope in 2009 overall. I loved being in the city, being able to get so much fresh air while performing a genuinely enjoyable job, being able to keep in touch with my friends from afar, and having my parents' house as a safe haven and an easy (though hopefully temporary!) commute. It truly gave me a lot of hope that good things were on the horizon.

Baby, I Need Your Lovin'

After I quit my data analytics job in Pharma, I was able to take that job at Wharton. It felt like a no-brainer (yes, that is another pun, and yes, you are welcome once again). I had prayed for purpose outside of a stressful corporate job, and I got one. Jim was starting his residency at UMDNJ, and since we had saved enough money while living with my parents, we were able to purchase and move into our first house in Deptford in August of 2009. Not only did I get the purpose I prayed for in my newfound work, but it was at this time that I also found out that I was two months pregnant with Reagan—a real miracle considering the timing of all my seizures from 2008 and with how little Jim and I were getting to see each other with his work schedule (70-80 hours a week, bless his gigantic heart!).

I remember the day that I found out that I was pregnant, too. It was August 18—I had worked a normal day like every other day and was supposed to stay in Philly, not at the new house that night. I had some more work that needed to be done, but that was all about to change. I went to the pharmacy down the street (walking distance is amazing) to pick up my good old regularly scheduled seizure medication (what else, right?), and while I was waiting, I happened to look over and see that pregnancy tests were on sale...how could I possibly skip an opportunity to save money on a sale like that? Who knows why they were on sale? Maybe they were defective, I have no idea.

After a mental boxing match trying to figure out why exactly they would have been on sale, I figured I could just buy them since my cycles had not really been tracking properly for a few months (perhaps due to the medication change, but I didn't care, because by the grace of God, my seizures were stable). And, although Jim and I had been trying and hoping that a baby might be in our future, we weren't sure if the timing was right and still felt somewhat uneasy and extra cautious about my stability with all the seizures and whatnot. Little did we know what miracle was on the path He had already mapped out for us.

I was at the house on Addison Street, all by myself when I took the test, which, in case you haven't guessed by now, came out positive! I remember being in an absolute sense of disbelief, but also thanking God! All the angels and my Mom Mom, Babci—anyone I could think of—I was praying and thanking for this amazing gift of a new life to join our family! This was a miracle. No question about that. I promised right then and there that I would do everything within my control to keep this baby safe. I was going to make sure this baby was happy and healthy and was not going to be in want of anything. Now, I had to gather myself so that I could get over the bridge to New Jersey to our new house which we could now (God willing) fill with a brand-new baby!

That ride to Deptford seemed to take forever! I don't think I listened to anything other than the prayers in my heart and head that this wasn't just a dream, and that it was all real. I knew I would need to wait until I got closer to home to call Jim because he would likely get worried that something was wrong. I was, after all, supposed to be staying in Philly that night, and usually, when I'm calling about something last minute or unexpected, it's presumed to be seizure-related, so I decided to wait. I waited until I was right around the corner, called Jim, and told him to meet me in the driveway.

Jim's first response was to ask me why he needed to meet me in the driveway. I told him to just do it, I had something to show him! A quick note about Jim, he's a big car enthusiast, so with my request, he very likely thought I'd gone out and bought a new car. I mean, why else would I want to surprise him in the driveway? Then again, we had just bought a new house...so unless we'd won the lottery, there was no way I would have bought a new car! But this was so much better, yeah, a new baby.

New babies are way better than new cars, right? RIGHT?! And hey, new babies and new cars have a lot in common. You gotta wash 'em, drive in the car with 'em carefully, and they require a lot of maintenance. But new cars absolutely cannot fill your heart with the same sense of purpose as a little life given to you from above. I had a feeling Jim would be excited about this surprise! So, when I got into the driveway, I rolled down the window and showed him the positive test.

To say he was perplexed would be an understatement. "What does this say?!?!" It took him a minute to process. And when he began finally being able to speak, it wasn't even more than just jumbled words. It was cute. "Is this? Are you? Are we?" Of course, just to be sure, I went inside with Jim and took another test (on sale, remember?). Just because I wasn't entirely sure that these sale pregnancy tests weren't defective, I also made Jim go out and get some fancy new digital ones...IN A CRAZY THUNDERSTORM! Sure enough, three fancy digital tests and then an even fancier blood test the next day, and it was all confirmed—this blessing was absolutely for real!

It is such a fascinating thing to know how intentional God is with the way He orchestrates our lives. I remember earlier that summer I had been upset because I didn't think I was ever going to get pregnant. I was at a friend's wedding when I found out that Jim's brother and sister-in-law were expecting their second child (Jim had forgotten to tell me, which made the whole situation that much more difficult to handle). My seizure medication had also caused me to lose a lot of weight, which made my cycles entirely unpredictable. It was difficult, at that time, to imagine being able to move into our new house without any real hope of filling it up with little children that we could love and raise!

It seemed only fair that since I was free of seizures at the time, I should be able to get pregnant immediately, especially since we were in the process of buying the house. I felt that it would only be right, that we sort of deserved it for all we had gone through. Patience, however, is a quality that can be so very elusive when it comes to these big types of things. This is a lesson I've especially had to learn as God is the ultimate master orchestrator directing with each step along the way. I just needed to learn to fully trust in His timing, His tempo, especially as I walked through stretches of waiting that sometimes felt painful and discouraging.

Being patient, though not my favorite thing in the world, is something I am able to do when needed and tested. It has not always been easy but taking a step back and looking at my life through each step, I can see how it has been divinely coordinated to get me to the places I have needed to go through the years. I have learned that I am merely playing the music in the opera that He has so distinctly mapped out for my life, and sometimes I play, but sometimes I must simply practice and learn the music.

My prayers may not always be answered in the way that I want them to be, or at the time that I want them answered, and honestly, sometimes it seems as though I am going through tremendous trials that are very faith-testing. Sometimes it feels that my journey is an uphill battle—but it could be so much worse. I must remember that everything is happening for a reason, and at the end of the day, I can rest easy knowing that God has heard me. As Jesus states so beautifully in Mark 11:24, "'Whatever you ask for in prayer, believe that you have received it, and it will be yours.'" You have not had "it" in the exact form you initially asked for, or even at the exact moment you desired for "it" to come to you. But that is okay.

One can't expect prayer for wealth to manifest itself in winning the million-dollar jackpot lottery, but perhaps God bestows upon you a wealth of blessings that are intangible, so unique and so vastly priceless that you don't realize just how rich your life really is. Finding those pockets of peace requires me to take a step back to realize that His plan is designed so intricately and that the opera of His perfect plan will be revealed at the right time, in the right place, and through His sometimes mysterious yet perfect ways.

I am merely the vessel, a singer to tell God's story that He has designed specifically for me. No matter how passionately we may want to pick up the pen and write our own story, that is not our ultimate given task, no. Instead, we are called to, plain and simple, just put the pen down and allow God to control the writing of His masterpiece of our lives. Allowing God the control that He has always had helps us to better reconcile with the peace that He desires for us.

Isn't that what the Blessed Mother did—put her complete trust in the Lord? Here she was, a virgin—suddenly pregnant and told, by the way, you are to have this baby, out of wedlock, and He will be the Savior, the King! She was likely a bit confused and thinking something like, *Wait, WHAT? I'm what? He's going to be WHO?* And in those ancient times, if you were even *living* out of wedlock, you could be stoned to death! But she had such faith in God's plan for her that she carried that baby Jesus *for us*! Now that is what I call trust! That is turning your will and life over to the path that is before you with open arms, an open mind, and an even more open heart.

Believing that love can conquer all, even the most daunting of fears, the goal, then, is to fully rely on God and know that He knows exactly what He is doing. Now, please understand that I do not by any stretch of the imagination consider myself on the same plane as our Blessed Mother. I continue to look to her as the quintessential example of trust, patience, and love. But I also know that while I may strive to be more like her, I am not her, and my struggles and circumstances will never be as remarkable as hers were. I simply use her as an example of how to approach life and the situations that God places before us.

I needed to understand that the idea is to trust without fear that God has selected each of my next steps entirely with my greater good in mind. With the orchestra image in mind, though, I wasn't the best player in the band, and I had to learn some really hard lessons along the way. They were lessons and trials that undoubtedly would only come to strengthen and prepare me for the next pieces of music placed in front of me. That isn't to say it was easy.

Going through the hard stuff is what makes the good stuff really great. As it has been said, life is both bitter and sweet, but it's the bitterness that makes the sweet that much sweeter. And I've been told that during the sweetness of life, you can say thank you and celebrate, whereas during those bitter times, you say thank you and learn and grow. Even if it takes time to stop and realize that you are growing in every step, as bitter as it may seem, as difficult as the *right now* is, it is still part of a *"gonna be great someday."*

Essential to my health and faith is the significance of remaining present in the here and now, as sensed moment by moment, and finding the cues to proceed along the next part of the song, the path, the life that He chose and created for us. If I find myself holding on to any moment once it is gone, I am unable to fully embrace the joys and lessons of the present. When your favorite song comes on the radio, can you really start to sing with the windows down, the wind blowing through your hair, sun shining on you while focusing on thoughts like *I really hated that last hour of music*? Of course not! Don't focus on the music that has already passed, stay focused instead on the music playing right now and sing out loud!

This mindful practice of remaining in the present and trusting without fear of what comes next is how we find the strength and the wisdom to be positive and grateful. And even though the story may be written and music orchestrated, it's not to say that I have no say whatsoever in my own fate. I can still believe in myself and my life's purpose. I can still wake up and choose to be empowered by thinking positively, by seeing the good, and by being strong. I can either stand up when I fall or stay knocked down. I can choose to take action in my life and keep moving forward. I am still the captain of my soul— He is the one who has built the ship and knows the ultimate destination.

I consistently prayed that somehow moving into this new home would make all our dreams come true. I made all the phone calls to close family and friends in those days following having found out about our pregnancy. It was such a wonderful gift to share this amazing blessing and news with all those we loved especially after the year we had experienced, the struggles and pains we had gone through. It was early September (the third, to be exact) that we found out I was already ten weeks along. If all stayed steady, we would get to meet our new baby at the end of March!

Despite the sheer excitement at the idea of meeting my baby, it was also nerve-racking. I was nervous at first as to how my seizure threshold would be impacted by pregnancy and if it could make me more susceptible to episodes. We weren't even sure at first if the medications were safe to take during pregnancy. Turns out, as we learned from the neurologists, that pregnancy can even sometimes offer a shield of protection from seizures because of the hormonal levels present. Even so, I still battled the worry about all my medications because, as I had come to learn clearly, anything could happen. We took the opportunity to call on all our angels for this beautiful miracle to come into the world safe and healthy, and for me to remain seizure-free for the duration of my pregnancy.

It was crazy to think that the same person who at eight years old had to be dragged, kicking and screaming, to church every week, was now regularly saying at least a million Hail Marys, and I had gotten to the point of having daily chats with God to thank Him for this amazing blessing. To see that every step and stumble along my journey was an opportunity to feel the blessings that God had given me. I thanked Him for giving me the chance to be a mama, despite my occasionally uncertain condition. I can remember thinking that there had to be a reason for all the craziness in my life. I firmly believed that God had (and still does, mind you) a plan for me, and at this point, being a mom did feel like part of that plan. So, He wouldn't just take it away, right?

A lot of things were happening all at the same time, and it couldn't be a coincidence. We had just moved into the new house; I was at that time seizure-free. Yep, definitely knocked on all possible wood surfaces at every opportunity. God wouldn't just pull the rug out from underneath us. So, I continued taking my meds, I consistently prayed, and I trusted that God was doing exactly what He was supposed to, and I thanked Him every single day that I honestly had nothing to fear at all. I was careful with each step on and off the Septa bus. I followed every bit of wisdom and advice on pregnancy for epileptics that I could find. And then we just patiently waited. Not an easy thing to do, but our baby would be worth the wait for sure.

On the anxiety front, though, it wasn't just me who had those worried feelings. Jim was nervous, too. I will say, though, despite his anxieties, he was the quintessential doting father-to-be! He did everything he could to accommodate my pregnancy moods and my weird but awesome cravings. I remember one night he went above and beyond. I had been through a pretty bad day after a long week at work, and he ordered Chinese food for dinner for us. I'd already decided I didn't want any because I wasn't in the mood, so he told the restaurant that he'd pick it up. The problem was, when he went to get it, my belly and the little baby I was growing decided that it wanted Moe's tacos which was right next door, a telling sign of just how much Reagan would come to love Taco Tuesday nights!

I was willing to be the one to go get in line at Moe's, but Jim was walking back to the car, noticing that he'd gotten a phone call that the food was being delivered by accident. The delivery guy was already waiting at the house, so we didn't really have time for me to get my Moe's tacos. When we got home, the Chinese food had been left on the doorstep (I guess we didn't need to be home after all). I was crushed. We had left Moe's for no reason! We could have gotten it, and I ended up crying and crying. It was weird but also normal that I was so sad about food. Before I could say anything more, Jim, the absolute hero of the story, left to go back to Moe's to get those tacos...and *even* waffle fries from Chick-fil-A because that is the kind of all-star Jim is, and that is one of the many reasons I love him so much!

Walking Miles, Baby Smiles, and Stresses Compile

Even though we were excited and ready to meet this miracle child, we still had months to go. It was a very long winter but walking around the campus was great for me and the baby while also taking my mind off all the many uncertainties still ahead. Taking breaks from work during lunch for these walks was beneficial, and I especially got a lot of walking done that November when Septa, the Southeastern Pennsylvania Transportation Authority, was on strike. I even decided to walk home from work in University City all the way to Society Hill at 38th and Walnut (look it up, that's impressive for a woman who is also a pregnant epileptic). I did a little walking during the days after the snowstorms, too. Traffic was a mess, and the buses were all re-routed because the streets were not being plowed, so walking was a real treat.

And speaking of plowing, we had one wild and crazy winter that year with unbelievable amounts of snow, even by the sub-freezing standards of Pennsylvania. It wouldn't be until later that I was able to determine what a real winter looks like in Upstate New York. Not much later, we had an incredibly huge storm just before Christmas, and thinking I was doing something awesomely helpful, I even tried to shovel some of the snow from the driveway because Jim was already working so hard at the hospital and then using the rest of his free time to sleep because of those ridiculous hours. Evidently, it is frowned upon for a pregnant lady with epilepsy to shovel snow, and I heard some stern words about it...I mean...what? Try and overdo everything and be independent? Who? Me? I would *never*...maybe.

There were several smaller storms after that, but the long winter forced a lot of time inside, which gave us the prime opportunity to get the house ready for the baby! We were even fortunate to have Jim's mom around to help us. She is a brilliant artist, and she painted the baby's room with a breathtaking and one-of-a-kind gorgeous wall-length mural with baby jungle animals. It was all so exciting, and by the early spring, everyone was getting eager to meet the new baby. It was anxiety-inducing but exhilarating all at the same time. We had no idea when the baby would come, and our patience was running thin because of the hope of the joy that was to come.

When the time came, I tried pushing for twenty-four hours (yes, you read that right...a full day!), but the baby simply wouldn't come out! Turns out I was not born with birthing hips, and our sweet tiny bundle of joy was a little bigger than we had expected. All that to say, all of our consistent and continuous prayers were answered on March 30, when our precious Reagan Marie was born. She weighed in at a healthy eight pounds and fourteen ounces. Talk about a sturdy baby! She was perfect, and while we felt far from perfect, we knew that we were perfect for her. We were utterly over the moon in love with every aspect of her, and we knew that she was a genuine gift from God, and we felt blessed to be given the opportunity to be her parents.

Reagan was the first grandchild for my parents and the first granddaughter for Jim's parents. So, she was doted on and adored endlessly. I was totally and completely enamored by every single inch of her not-so-tiny self. It was not lost on me how much of a gift from God she was. She was born with such a pleasant demeanor, and she made the first-time mom experience so enjoyable! Since she was an easy baby most of the time, I decided to try and get back into a rhythm of life after my maternity leave was done, so I opted for a part-time schedule, in part to put aside the fear that I'd be wasting my degree if I were to just stay at home.

I was able to negotiate a return to work on a part-time basis in June, but deep down I knew that I just couldn't be stressed out going back and forth traveling over the bridge so often, risking getting stuck in traffic on the Expressway on Route 42 in addition to worrying about who would be picking up Reagan in the case of an emergency. It was one thing if Jim was working a traditional 9-5 job, but in the end, it seemed that I was trying to do it all on my own. I was managing a lot of the responsibilities at home on top of working and being the brand-new mama bear, as well.

Dinners, groceries, cleaning, bills, and laundry fell upon my shoulders most of the time, typically without the help of my co-pilot, which eventually became somewhat overwhelming. All of that was enough for me to consider justifying staying home, but then add that I also had to worry about my seizure disorder, as well. Thankfully, it was under control, but it was still constantly in the back of my mind. The level of stress that was caused by work was within our control, and it just didn't make sense to continue allowing that stress to infiltrate my mind.

We were so fortunate to be able to afford the luxury of my staying home as a full-time mama. There was no price tag that we could place on my health, especially during these amazing formative years for Reagan as she got to stay in my care instead of someone else's. We were willing to make whatever financial sacrifice we needed to for me to be present for our new bundle of joy. If I did not have epilepsy, then maybe things would have been different, maybe I could have done the working mom thing like so many others have done, but I had to accept the fact that I was simply not like every other mom.

God created me exactly as He did with this condition so that I could use my life and my circumstances to be of service to others in His name, though I hadn't yet figured out exactly how I was meant to fulfill such potential and I certainly didn't want to ruin my chances. I didn't want to wait until something terrible happened to say to myself that it was all too much. I knew in my heart that I needed to step back and take it easy with some of the things in my life.

Coming to that decision, again, was another one of those no-brainers for me. Yes, it was a difficult decision to make, but I knew in my heart that it was the right thing to do. People must make sacrifices all the time because of health problems, working spouses, and single parenting. Throughout life we make sacrifices, each one feeling more significant than simply letting go of the measly position I held at work for my baby.

Despite what felt like a simple decision, it still plagued my mind. Why wasn't I able to do the seemingly simple job of multi-tasking my life? Others do it all the time. Others feel no sense of anxiety or overwhelming fear when they do it. Why was this such a difficult choice for me to be able to make? I had reason and logic on my side. I even had the necessary tools in my toolbox of life, helping me know the best ways to prioritize, and this was the only real solution. I had to follow this new path. It might have taken some time to get my head and my heart to align, but they eventually did, and it was the best choice I ever made.

Because of this, I got to enjoy each moment with our not-so-little darling since I didn't have to go to work anymore.

We got to spend an extended amount of time at my parents' beach house at the Jersey shore. We both got spoiled, and I got much-appreciated love and support from friends and family. My heart was full, and I was so grateful, but at the same time, as time went on, I couldn't help but feel a little bit off somehow. It felt that while I had made the right decision, there was something blocking the joy from my heart, and I couldn't feel the happiness that was once there.

It felt as though I couldn't experience joy. Consider it something like a clogged artery. All the right pieces are there, but there is something blocking the ability for it all to work properly and in the way that God intended. My heart and my head were clogged, and I could not recognize the joy that was right in front of me. We had almost as soon forgotten about my seizures, and I was getting to fulfill my promise to be a great mama, but there was still a dark cloud that had come and rested above me. I could sense that something was about to happen…

It was in October of 2010 that the dark clouds of life started to pour heavy rain upon me. I had a seizure that month, and then I had two more significant ones in April of 2011. It turns out that the dark cloud was just the beginning of a mighty big storm of postpartum depression. While sitting in that storm, I saw more clearly a path that I had turned down a long time ago…one that now presented itself as a fork with no outlet. And it was in these moments that I fell into the trap of "If I only had a brain," treating the pain of my postpartum depression with the worst possible medication: self-medication.

Bad Medicine

To self-medicate for a person with a family history of alcoholism will always end poorly. That negative ending only gets worse and more dangerous when factoring in a medical condition such as epilepsy. Over the course of time, I kept making the wrong choices that kept pushing me closer and closer to the edge of destruction. Things were well on the way to a very poor ending for me. How poor, you ask? So poorly that I ended up in rehab twice. So poorly that on December 7, 2012, the person I loved more than anything in the world, my soulmate, my Jim, filed for divorce.

It wasn't long before he had filed when we had basically the entire world in our hands. For having such a good head on my shoulders and with so much to live for, I knew better than to make such careless choices that could ruin everything and risk losing it all. And yet I ended up in rehab and in AA uttering the painful words that many before me, and may since have said, "Hello, my name is Marisa, and I'm an alcoholic." It is something that clearly did not happen overnight. Perhaps it was a culmination of all those fears of failure that built up in my heart over the years. Perhaps it was all that, coupled with the postpartum depression that caused the bubble of my life to finally burst.

I had given up on myself and lost sight of my faith and my family. I had to face the painful truth that I am an alcoholic, though that is just a small part of who I am. These are both diseases, epilepsy and alcoholism. This is something I needed to learn, and the only way I could learn it was by hitting absolute rock bottom. And rock bottom is exactly what I hit, and I hit it about as hard as possible. We make a lot of mistakes in life, and there are a lot of things that change us and make us who we are. For me, the darkness of this period is just one of those fortunate mistakes that needed to happen.

I had been a casual drinker since I was in my early twenties (twenty-one, to be exact, thank you to the government of the United States), and admittedly, I had a lot of the good and responsible fun of partying during my senior year of college with some of the greatest roommates of all time. But it was determined early on that even a single glass of wine or one beer could impact the efficacy of my seizure medication and put me at risk for further seizures, so I went from casual drinking to no drinking at all, for my own health. And I hope it goes without saying that I had not been drinking while I was pregnant with Reagan. But it is a disease, an addiction, and it is one that I struggled deeply with and needed to learn to navigate in a healthy and appropriate way.

This disease of alcoholism took a very deep and ugly root in my insecurities. I guess I always felt an inherent pressure to be the best, to perform the best, and to show the world that I was everything I was supposed to be. Even winning second place still meant being the first loser, which was entirely defeating. In the same way, getting a B on an exam always meant I should have studied harder and longer. There was even a song I listened to as a teenager, and it always caused me to pause as it basically said that we will always be loved just as we are, but only if what we are is perfect. No one ever expected perfection from me, but I unfortunately put that pressure upon myself.

During these formative years, however, God gave me the most loving and supportive parents. They never punished me if I did not perform up to certain expectations (usually my own). After the very few times I heard those painful speeches of "we're disappointed in you," I did my best to avoid them. I adopted the mentality of avoiding failure and being seen as a disappointment at all costs, going above and beyond to do my best and to be perfect. Those feelings were not because of anyone else, though. Those feelings were because of my own expectations that I had placed upon myself.

My friends and family only ever wished for me to simply be myself, and they showed me support and kindness. It is said that comparison is the thief of joy, and my goodness…I didn't need anyone else; I could just compare myself to the ideal image of myself, and I was my own harshest critic. I would beat myself up and depress myself just thinking about the fact that I wasn't perfect, and it would create pain and sadness.

I had yet to learn that perfection was an unrealistic standard, demonic even. Excellence and perfection are definitely not one and the same. And excellence was a much more realistic, attainable, and even gratifying standard. Not to mention better for my mental and physical health.

Knowing that I had not lived up to my own expectations of this unrealistic perfection was devastating, and I struggled to learn how to make sense of it all and what I should do or where I should go with my unwarranted feelings of failure. I felt lost and in a distinctly miserable state of mind.

As a kid, I'd done a pretty good job staying out of trouble in school. I excelled in my classes and was, by all accounts, a geek. I got straight A's and was an honor student. All in all, a very well-rounded kid. I was even a cheerleader—

well, sort of. I was the school mascot, the roar-some and mighty cougar! I was a four-year starting varsity catcher, I ranked in the state. I was in student government and on the prom committee, I was a Girl Scout, and I never once got detention. I was so strait-laced I didn't even cut school on Senior Ditch Day. Then I went on to graduate from Wharton! I married a doctor! I had achieved excellence by all standards, right?!?! Through my own distorted mirror, though, I hadn't achieved that demonic level of unrealistic perfection, and it would end up leading me down a terrible path of self-destruction.

All throughout my life, my parents could not have been prouder of me. On my side of things, though, I could not have been more terrified of letting them down or being seen as a failure in some way. I had not yet internalized the message of love and hope that God loved me no matter what I did, even in my perfect imperfections. After years of carrying the weight of avoiding letting anyone down, the combination of postpartum depression and the return of my seizures in late 2010 followed by more the next spring, I felt overwhelmed and overburdened. I knew that I was depressed...I was a depressed alcoholic.

I remember the first time I ever got pulled over for drunk driving was when I was seventeen years old. I had only had my license for two weeks. I wasn't drunk. I hadn't even had my first taste of alcohol yet. I just so happened to be swerving in my lane while I was trying to get toll money out for the Ocean Drive Bridge between Ocean City and Sea Isle. I have never been pulled over for drunk driving ever since—which means I've never technically been pulled over for drunk driving—only suspected drunk driving because of a silly misunderstanding. I tried to make good decisions; I was always cautious. I didn't want to risk throwing all the positivity in my life away.

There were occasionally times when I had containers of alcohol open in the car, though, despite not drinking in those moments. Yet, I still managed to avoid trouble in those instances. I didn't even go out with a fake ID until just a couple of months before my twenty-first birthday, and even then, I got caught within thirty seconds of taking my first sip of a margarita.

You might think I'd have taken all of these as warning signs and hints from God that I simply shouldn't mess around with alcohol at all. There was always a slight lingering fear that alcohol could possibly be a problem in my life—both of my grandfathers were alcoholics, and my hard-partying Irish Catholic family could easily fill trashcans full of empty bottles every single weekend. I was very familiar with the idea of people having just "a few too many." I just never thought it would be me.

The Jagged Cliffs Overlooking Rock Bottom

When I was younger, I worked summers in Sea Isle City making smoothies on the boardwalk, and I rarely ever broke curfew. It wasn't until I was seventeen that I figured out how to sneak out of my parents' house by climbing over the railing on the deck and onto the roof of their car. Then down the sidewalk I would go, and just hang out with friends at the beach or some older guys somewhere. It was around that time, when I was seventeen, that I had my first drink, as well.

I should have stayed away from that initial drink, of course, but it was eventually the fourth or fifth that officially did me in and left me with a horrifically memorable hangover the next day. My boss at the smoothie shop insisted that I work the blender on ultra-high, which did not help the headache at all–he wanted me to learn my lesson, too. Unfortunately, that would also not be my last hangover.

As with many youths, a lot of my fears, insecurities, and resentments grew to exceeding strength and festered within me during my college years. It became a very challenging time for me—Ivy League business school was no walk in the park, but I worked just as I partied. Partying ultimately became a relief— I often felt the need to rebel, and it seemed to be okay because everyone else was doing it, too, and I was still managing to get good grades. Looking back, though, I can see that I was mostly just drinking as a normal college kid would with a college kid mindset. In hindsight, this is obviously not the greatest thing in the world to do.

It is clear to me now, but at the time, I was not taking enough care of my mental health. How very blessed I was that my aunt happened to work on campus at Penn in the Department of Student Health Services. She and I had become quite close over the years, and it worked out entirely to both of our benefit for me to be able to have her as an on-campus resource when I needed to get away from the stresses of student life. She always provided comfort and a familiar face, and she often reassured me that my feelings were all normal and that things would be okay. She really was the best!

I honestly do not know how I would have managed those several years without her. Sure, I could have gone to student health services on my own, but having her familiar face, someone who already knew me so well, made everything that much more valuable. She is a true inspiration. Her work in the field of mental health has always been tremendously valuable, and she continues to be a source of great love, guidance, and support. She is still one of my favorite go-to people in times of stress and difficulty.

While my Aunt Kate was able to provide the best advice, I think I can see now that I should have reached out more frequently to her about the struggles going on deep down, especially considering that her area of expertise is in the field of substance abuse counseling. And here I was that whole time, thinking and maybe even pretending that I was doing totally fine. It was during this same time that both my grandmothers were passing away, one after the other, of alcohol-related complications...and then my own mother started to show traits that I had never noticed before...

I saw her at times overindulgent and sloppy, and I worried for her. I would come to question if she had her own insecurities that she was trying to escape from, and I swore to myself I would be better at coping. It gave me even more conviction, then, to be wary of the power that alcohol could possibly hold over me. When my grandmother passed away from pancreatic cancer, I made it a point to stay aware and alert of the various medical dangers of drinking in excess given our family history.

Despite all that, or maybe because of all that, I was not a super heavy drinker as college went on. I had to work hard to keep my grades up, and I decided I never wanted to be "that girl" at the parties. I never woke up in a stranger's bed, and I was sensible enough to keep strangers out of mine. I believe I was quite funny and charming when I partied, but I also made sure to stay responsible. That is, of course, until I turned twenty-one and was legally allowed to purchase my own alcohol, which led to me buying, and hiding, alcohol, because I was living off-campus in a house with seven other girls, and as loving as I may be, I wasn't sure I wanted them to know or judge me for how much I was drinking on my own by comparison.

Even with the secrecy of my drinking in those days, I made some of the best friends of my life that year. These were all ladies who are still in my life and have been with me through all the highs as well as the deeply troubling lows. We have always had each other's backs and have gotten through weddings, divorces, births, and deaths. This undeniably wonderful, not to mention brilliant, group of ladies would always come to my aid (and occasionally have) at a single moment's notice. They have always been like sisters to me. I do not regret for a single second the decision that I made to live with them that year even if I did lack good judgement. In all His divine wisdom, God put us all together for a reason.

That said, it is clear to me now that some of my behavior back then was rooted in the mindset of an alcoholic. This is when I began exhibiting alcoholic symptoms (unbeknownst to me of course) such as the needing vs. wanting, the craving vs. indulging. During my senior year of college, I made some epically bad decisions. Okay, maybe not apocalyptically bad, but definitely unwise. That season of my life began to exemplify the Scarecrow mentality of "If I only had a brain," only this time, unfortunately, it was of my own choosing.

I made choices that could be attributed to being young and dumb, but then throw a bit of alcohol into that mix, and I was doing stupid stuff that I would never have previously considered as a responsible and strait-laced kid. Things like piercing my nose and staying out way too late every night of the week. It was hard enough to keep up with the rest of the Ivy Leaguers, and I should have known better than to potentially risk it all by going out so much and doing other unwise things like blowing off my classes and stopping eating regularly.

When the dust of my thoughts all settled, it was clear that I was all over the place and an absolute mess. But an alcoholic? That couldn't be me. I was definitely too smart to allow myself to get to that point. Or so I thought. Luckily, once I started as a data analyst for Johnson & Johnson, I didn't have the ability or freedom to keep living that college life anymore.

For a long while, being married to Jim and being regularly warned that my seizure medication would be negatively affected by alcohol seemed to settle me into a more "normal" and even "casual" relationship with drinking...like a traditional relationship of maybe a drink every now and again after work. It all just seemed to be working properly, and everything seemed to be totally under control. But that's exactly the thing: it was all part of God's master plan as the almighty conductor of life to bring me more entirely and completely closer to Him through this.

You might look at this situation and think there is a massive contradiction here. How could I say I was a woman of such faith and trust in God that my epilepsy would be fine, but then actively make the decision to drink myself slowly and gradually out of control? You see, that's just it, though. I needed to learn a very valuable lesson about that very thing: CONTROL. I needed to feel that rock bottom, to lose complete control and feel the powerlessness, in order to learn how important it was that I fully turn myself and my will over to God on a daily basis. I needed to walk through these uncomfortable and hurtful things in order to prepare for the true challenges that were to lie ahead.

You might be wondering, though, how does such a thing like alcoholism happen after what seems like such a positive go of things? It's not like I woke up one day and thought, "I'm really not outta control...and this cliff isn't so far up, and rock bottom couldn't possibly hurt that bad, could it?" No, like anything else that is as epically terrible as this, it took time to reach that point. It was like a bad seed that decided to take root, and I just kept feeding it over the years. I just kept climbing my way up the cliff one bad decision at a time. I could have been anything I wanted, I could have climbed the corporate ladders of many different companies, but instead, I kept slowly climbing my way up the cliff to becoming an alcoholic.

While the senior year partying did simmer down a bit after college, I still attended the occasional margarita happy hour with co-workers and friends. And then it became more happy hours. And then I'd be going to happy hour alone. While Jim and I were already married at this point, he was so busy with med school in Long Island that he didn't see the fact that I was careening past casual drinker territory and swerving heavily into having a serious problem. He didn't know I was drinking solo from a hidden stash in the closet every day after work.

I would find and use any excuse I could to justify drinking. I didn't just stop at, "Hey, it's a wedding, we should celebrate." No, I used everything. It was a bad day at work, and I just needed to unwind. Drink. Jim was working long hours, and I was feeling lonely. Drink...it was a ruthless and ugly cycle. Looking back now, I know it was wrong, and I know it was unhealthy, but I will not deny having done it because every season of our lives is orchestrated by God. The good times *and* the bad times. It is how we respond in those times that determines and shapes us. While my initial responses in those moments might not have been great, I stand here now as an example of learning from my mistakes.

I will say, when we did finally get pregnant, it's worth celebrating that I actively chose to enjoy that season alcohol-free because we were just so blessed and excited to have been given such a gift...and it's not like I was an actual alcoholic or anything...I could stop...but then WHOA...after the baby came, I felt like I was kind of doing the (semi) single parenting thing while Jim was at the hospital all the time (absolutely grateful for him and for his job, but that doesn't mean the hard time was any less hard). Occasionally, drinking was the encouragement I felt I needed in those tough times by myself. Then the infamous postpartum depression kicked in and triggered a deep depression, and my need for alcohol returned. It became so easy to keep writing off the drinking as a need because of all these excuses and insecurities. However, I was ignoring the root of my pain.

I invented all these excuses and all these issues that needed to be filled with the distraction of alcohol. Sure, a lot of these issues and insecurities were real, but I was choosing to not deal with them, and only dull them with the numbing nature of alcohol, while still being able to walk that fine line of not getting drunk. These things weren't going to go away if I kept drinking and trying to numb it all away. I made excuses all the time...the game was on, the baby was still crying...but hey, I could bargain, too. I'll stop drinking tomorrow, one more drink today isn't going to hurt anyone.

Even better, I would decide, I'll only drink on the days that end in "Y," right (that's all the days, just to be clear)! I can choose to stop if it starts affecting my work. I would make all these secret promises to myself...but then I just kept on drinking alone and in secret. I'm still a good parent, my baby is cared for and healthy. I still cook dinner almost every night of the week. I can stop if Jim finds my hidden stash. If the "real" doctors tell me it is a problem, then I'll stop. If it gets in the way of being a parent or an employee, that will be it.

All the while, I was living in total denial of the fact that going to six different liquor stores in the same week to buy boxed wine was a genuine problem. I was functional, too! I thought to myself, *I've absolutely got this!* I was an Ivy League grad, after all, so of course I could balance my drinking, parenting, and working all with zero issues! That is, until it *was* a problem. That is, until it affected my epilepsy, and I was back to having those awful seizures again. That is, until it started to affect Jim, too. God just kept throwing at me all the many reasons I shouldn't be drinking, but I ignored them. For every good reason God gave me not to drink, I found excuses *to* drink because I was doing a great job with the whole balancing act of it all.

It might be safe to think that I would be of the mindset to never want to pick up a drink again, plain and simple, out of fear of re-engaging my epileptic episodes or even because of my huge responsibilities as a new parent, and that would be a reasonable thought process. As an alcoholic, though, I always found a way to justify my reckless behavior. I could be well in control with medication for the most part, and as I eventually discovered after rather unwise and irresponsible experimentation, it was relatively safe to take my medication with alcohol. And since this season of my life was tough, as a semi-single parent feeling lonely while Jim was away at work, those were the straws that broke this camel's back, so to speak.

All my bargaining and justification came to a height of stupidity when Reagan was about three months old, and we had an almost-full bottle of wine in the back of the fridge. My anxiety levels were through the roof, struggling to decide whether to become a full-time mom or keep working, feeling anxious about our finances, and missing Jim because of his work schedule...I was overwhelmed.

I didn't have my mom to help...I was having a hard time being a new mom...so I started checking my breastfeeding schedule and planning my sips of wine around that curated timeframe. Then I continued making that allowance for myself and going back for more sips every day that week. The next week, I went and bought another bottle, and as Jim's hours got longer, and when Reagan was no longer dependent on me for food...I took even more of those sips.

Ironically, each time I got to go see my family at the beach and witnessed how out of control some of my own family members could be, it caused me to keep taking more sips, not less. No matter how irrational it might have felt or seemed at the time. Seeing other people sloppy made me resentful and made me want to drink. I just kept justifying and negotiating and bargaining with myself over those choices and that behavior. I would secretly pack water bottles of vodka. I would make sure to pack wine for vacations. I always had Listerine and Halls for every trip to the bathroom to help cover up my secret drinking. I actively kept choosing all of this, despite knowing it could be jeopardizing my baby and my risk of having seizures return!

I kept up this secretive behavior for a whole year, thinking I had everyone fooled. I put on a bubbly and loving mask of a new mom, attentive wife, and thoughtful daughter...on the outside everything was fine. For me, on the inside, though...fine meant **F**aithless, **I**rresponsible, **N**egligent, and **E**gocentric. On the inside, I was terribly insecure, scared, and filled with resentment. I was an unworthy mess who couldn't figure out how to stop. I felt I needed alcohol to keep myself going. I needed it to feel ready to tackle my mountains of responsibility, to feel smart, to feel worthy, and to numb myself from the pain and loneliness of missing my overworked husband. I needed the alcohol to numb the fear of failing as a mom.

The ironic part of that, obviously, is that the fear of failing as a mom led me to drink, which in turn made me a terribly irresponsible mom. I had to continue numbing myself from the ever-present fear of letting my Wharton degree go to waste and, even worse, letting my parents down. As I started to drink earlier and earlier, I ended up getting sloppier and sloppier. I picked irrelevant and ugly battles with Jim, and then it became clear to him that I had been hiding my drinking from him all this time.

Jim begged me to stop and get help. It was very clear I needed it, and despite knowing I needed it, I was not ready to admit to my family that I was exactly what I had feared all along...a failure. That I had absolutely screwed everything in my life up. I had never screwed up my life before, and it only figures that the first time I really did screw up, I did so to epic proportions. I had been trying to push down so many fears and resentments with alcohol, I'd eventually lost sight of how much damage I was doing to everything and everyone all around me. All my fears were coming true. I had hurt my husband and put my daughter in danger far too many times than I could admit.

One Step Forward...

In the summer of 2011, both my and Jim's parents decided to come and stage an intervention. When I refused to leave, Jim took our daughter to his parents' house, telling me that if I wanted to see her, I would have to enter the treatment facility in Princeton the following night, no questions. It all became so very real, the pain and the natural consequences of a long string of terrible choices had led me to that very moment. So, on August 18, 2011, right around noon, I took my final drink. At 8 p.m. that same night, I entered the Carrier clinic.

I naively thought that that would be it. I detoxed, and I was super proud of myself for having completed such an intense outpatient program. I declared myself an alcoholic and started working through the process. Oh, how truly painful it was to admit that word out loud. Alcoholic. That first public meeting served as an absolute ego-crushing moment, having to admit that in front of strangers. Because admittance of the problem is the first step, and me being a rule follower, going step by step and following this first one made sense. Admit that I had a problem, okay, done. Got that out of the way, said the words, said it all out loud, and went to the meeting. I was already hitting home runs with this sobriety thing!

But was I really? Sure, I did the admittance thing, I went to the meetings, worked the steps, and followed the program. By all accounts, I was doing it right—and might I add, all while keeping my seizures at bay, not having one for eight whole months! I was sober for those eight months, too. Jim was proud of me; my family was proud of me—everything was exactly how it should be. But was it really? Why would I second guess such positive progress in such a good direction? Well, why did this all begin in the first place? Right...it was because Jim found my hidden stash. It was because Jim asked me to go through the treatments. Of course, I could choose to be sober since he asked me to. It was like giving up chocolate for Lent.

Being able to achieve something within a timeframe like this, and to reach the goal that someone else has set for you with no real defined benefit in mind for yourself, of course that was doable. More important than that, I simply didn't want to be a disappointment. Because, well, going back to that ugly seed that had taken root, feeling like a disappointment was a big reason why I was drinking in the first place...so was fear...and insecurity...and resentment. And, to be real, I kind of resented the entire intervention process, and the fact that I was forced into having nothing but supervised visitations with MY OWN daughter! What kind of a ridiculous situation that I couldn't even be trusted with my own daughter?! It was mind-blowing.

All these issues–fear, resentment, insecurity—yeah, they don't get tackled in the quick crash course outpatient stuff, and there was no Cliff's Notes version of the rehab I attended. I had yet to work on so many complex issues. Heck, I had yet to discover that fear, resentment, and insecurity were even part of my deepest triggers. That all might seem obvious now, being able to look back in hindsight, but at the time, I didn't know anything other than I was drinking too much! I had gained knowledge of the problem but had not become wise to my issues. And, as I have come to understand, knowledge and wisdom are vastly different.

You know that a tomato is technically a fruit, but you must be wise to keep it out of a fruit salad, right!? I had no idea that those deep-rooted feelings of fear and resentment triggered me to turn to drinking to numb those painful thoughts and feelings. I can see it all clearly now, but when I was right in the middle of it, it was too difficult to see that reality.

Facing Truth, Forcing Change, and Finding Acceptance

While I had said the word "alcoholic" to everyone else, I knew that I hadn't fully admitted it to myself. I came back home for eight months... and then that feeling began creeping up again, the resentment mostly, but also the bitterness. It was about this time that Jim and I started fighting... again. After a long eight months, the wheels, as they say, came off, because I was the one driving the bus again.

Fighting with Jim was just awful. He even flat-out told me that I was not bringing him happiness anymore. You can likely imagine how those words made me feel. And, of course, it led me to drink because I was caught up feeling lonely and like I'd messed up. I was just wrecked and had only myself to blame... and so I kept drinking. I was terrified, and the only way I knew to cope was with alcohol. Jim filed those divorce papers on December 7, and they served as the catalyst for finally accepting actual help.

With everything swirling around, seemingly out of control, I felt like I had no choice but to keep drinking and hiding it. I was so afraid my parents would find out and be mad that I'd fallen off the wagon after having done so well for such a long time. But, as time continued, I was drinking because I needed to forget everything that had happened, and I was feeling entirely pathetic. This brought on all kinds of questions and self-reflection.

Had I really addressed all (or any) of the underlying issues when I did the outpatient program? I had said all the words out loud and knew what the twelve steps were, but had I worked through any of them? Or was I just checking off the box to say I did it? I know we're all guilty of that at some point in our lives—simply checking the box of the task, but not actually accomplishing the intended goal.

We all have those days when we simply go to church to say we went to church, sure. But did you really pray? Were you emotionally and mentally present? If not, then what was the point? Just going to fill a seat? I spent a lot of my life simply checking various boxes doing what was asked of me. This time, by attending the outpatient program after the intervention because my family wanted me to, I didn't accomplish the goal of healing. I didn't achieve the mindset of actively trying to stop drinking, or more importantly, even, to figure out why I was trying to solve all my problems with alcohol despite knowing just how much I had to be thankful for.

Don't hear me wrong: I was absolutely terrified at the thought of going into long-term inpatient care! What would I do about my precious blessing, Reagan? Who would pay the bills and manage the house while Jim was working? What if I came out of the other side and Jim decided I wasn't worth the wait? But…but…there really was no question, the best thing to happen to me at that time in my life, and the one that finally made things "click" in my self-doubting mind was when a counselor simplified everything in the most powerful way possible.

He said to me, "Here is your life" (with his arms extended horizontally). He then said, "You are an incredibly smart woman, obviously having graduated from Penn, but you cannot just think your way out of this disease. This is ninety days (fingers pinched at a millimeter distance). You cannot have this (arms fully outstretched again, representing the rest of my life), without doing the self-work during this" (itty bitty space of ninety days of inpatient care).

That gave me the encouragement I needed, and I finally agreed to enter the "Changes for Women" inpatient ninety-day program at Seabrook House in South Jersey. Finally, I was faced with the opportunity and ability to get comfortable with being uncomfortable. Because growth and change usually don't happen without some level of discomfort. Think about any new exercise regimen and how sore you are the next day! But relearning the music God put before me, putting in the work, and digging through the soil to get to the roots of my triggers and emotional insecurities was hard work and required me to stretch my faith muscles.

While I was at Seabrook, I felt like I was finally able to focus. I could focus on myself; I could go deep into the "why" of it all. I finally started to work through the steps. I listened to the experts. I was able to stop trying to think my way out of the disease of alcoholism, and likely most importantly, I was able to rediscover my faith. Not just a simple faith of Bible- or Qur'an-thumping religiousness. It was a deep and genuine faith, one that could and absolutely would carry me through to learning how to be positive and look at the darkness from moments of my life and learn that God was there, and He was teaching me things that would help to sustain me later in life.

I am not a prophet or a preacher, and I am not one to believe that you must believe in God to have a program like this work. I do believe, however, that having faith of some sort, faith in a presence greater than ourselves who exists in the universe, is essential in establishing a foundation upon which we can build a framework of success, support, belief, and gratitude. It's not that I just rediscovered my faith in God while in rehab, no, I also was able to find faith in myself and because of that, I also discovered a newfound gratitude.

This stay at Seabrook was so entirely different than my first attempt at sobriety because the faith I found was transformational. Going back to the idea of Lent and having the willpower to give something up for a fixed period as a sacrifice at someone else's behest, this time I finally understood sobriety as something more than just willpower, just as Lent is more than just giving up chocolate. Lent at its core is about being tested while out of our comfort zone like Jesus was in the desert. The wheels fell off the bus after my eight months of sobriety the first go-round because I had failed the test in the desert of temptation by giving in to my fears and insecurities, instead of turning to prayer and trusting that I was going to be ok just being me.

I learned that I could be okay by simply being myself. And I was pretty excellent! Plus, everyone else was already taken, anyway. I was able to see once again that I was important, that I was someone of worth. I got to learn once, "By the grace of God I am what I am" (1 Corinthians 15:10). That is more than enough for His "'grace is sufficient'" and His "'power is made perfect in weakness'" (2 Corinthians 12:9). Then I realized all those insecurities were just voices in my head meant to keep me from becoming the person God put me on the planet to be. He intentionally made me the perfectly imperfect person that I am.

At Seabrook I learned that in those times of temptation to give up and give in to my fears and doubts, it was not a matter of willpower but only through turning to prayer, trusting in God, and turning to Him instead of the bottle for help that I could get my life back and keep it. In rehab, I finally learned to turn my will over, to choose faith instead of fear and temptation and I was making this change for myself, not because anyone was demanding it of me. I wanted to get through that desert more than anything and knew I would need His help. It was and is the reason I have been able to truly grasp sobriety and remain sober long-term.

Being able to choose faith over fear when tempted, truly choosing faith, instead of eating the chocolate in the desert was critical. And each day that I made it through another few steps in that desert, I was grateful to have survived with His blessings. I realized how much God had given me to live for and look forward to without alcohol, and I didn't even need chocolate either when I had such an incredibly sweet husband (remember that Chik-fil-A run??!) and precious daughter.

Most importantly, though, and this is one of the most essential points in getting me through the rest of the challenges that epilepsy would pose for me, is that I learned how important working the third step (trusting in a higher power) was and how valuable the serenity prayer would become in not just the rest of my journey but every single day of my life.

Do you remember that control I had been seeking for so long in so many places? Step three talks all about making the decision to turn our will and our lives over to the care of God. Basically, just telling Him, "Thy will be done." While I was at Seabrook, I found that although I had practiced faith growing up, going to church, repeating prayers at the proper time during Mass, participating in certain activities during holidays and whatnot, there was a huge difference between practicing faith, having faith, and being faith-filled.

Inpatient treatment taught me the significant lesson of how I could truly let go, letting God take over. Finding that true faith meant having the ability to put down the pen and learn the music while also knowing that God is the author and conductor. I would be held in the palm of His hands. This is one lesson I very much needed and was finally able to apply as my path continued to unfold after I completed inpatient treatment.

Amazingly, but by what I don't consider a coincidence, I remained seizure-free throughout my stay at Seabrook. This uninterrupted time was crucial in getting sober, getting mentally and emotionally healthy, and learning how to turn my will over to God daily. Somewhere between December 7 and March 23, I discovered that I wanted to be sober for ME, first and foremost! I wanted sobriety more than anything! It was discovering this that helped me to decide that I wanted to do everything in my power to make sure Reagan never followed in my footsteps as she grew up, as I had followed the footsteps that went before me, and so I knew I needed to be a better example.

For those unfamiliar, the serenity prayer goes a little something like this, "God, grant me the serenity to accept the things I cannot change, the courage to change the things that I can, and the wisdom to know the difference." Some may view the idea of acceptance in certain circumstances as a negative concession of sorts, as in, "Oh, it's just something I have to accept." Some might think of it as settling or conceding that there is no better option. Once I was able to truly surrender to the process of sobriety and recognize that my epilepsy diagnosis was beyond my control, I was better able to view the whole thing as positive and a particularly empowering tool that I could use.

I knew that I couldn't change my diagnosis. I have epilepsy, yes, but the diagnosis is entirely out of my control, always was and always will be. Accepting it—and I mean honestly and truly accepting it as God's will for me and then not being angry, frustrated, bitter, or resentful—it allowed me and my heart and mind to be more open to focus on so many more of the amazing blessings that have been consistently bestowed upon me. I have been blessed to learn that it doesn't take alcoholism or even epilepsy to put that beautiful prayer into play in my everyday life.

Just think about it—being able to free up your mental energy getting all frustrated about waiting in a long checkout line at the store because it is crowded and there aren't enough workers and then someone can't find their wallet in front of you. Can you suddenly open more lanes yourself? Can you make the person's wallet magically appear or make the cashier go faster? Okay, say this delay is causing you to be late for an important meeting and the person you are meeting is going to be super upset now that you are late.

So, what is in your control, then? The ability to call and complain about something? Once you get to the checkout, you should show gratitude to the person who is working (who is very likely overworked to begin with). If you are with your children, you get the honor of modeling patience and ingenuity while waiting by playing a game of tic-tac-toe with (if you're anything like me with a mom-purse) the back of your shopping list and a pen. If you are alone and it is a long wait, make that phone call to a lonely friend or elder relative who you know would just love to hear from you. Each of these moments is an opportunity to show those you love that you were thinking about them and putting your love and support into action.

You could get angry about circumstances that are completely out of your control, but doing so serves no purpose. Ranting and raving at the people around you only spreads toxicity and hate, which they are likely to keep spreading like a virus. As for those circumstances alluded to in the serenity prayer itself, when I ask for courage to change the things that I can, this is also an opportunity to change the negative into the positive. While I was unable to change my diagnosis, and I couldn't change the fact that I was facing wild surgery, I could change whether I was going to push people away or pull them in closer.

Then, as for knowing the difference between the things you can and cannot change, sometimes it is easier than others, but it certainly brings me peace to reflect inward and look upward, trying to truly discern the situations in or out of my control and whether they are worth my mental energy getting all worked up over. Are politics within my control Only to a certain extent, right? I can vote and I can work to get others to do the same, but the outcome is out of my control, isn't that right? So, when we try to control everything, we lose sight of the things that we can control and the peace that can come from that realization.

Not only did I want to prove myself to myself, to Jim, and to those who love and care about me, but I wanted our family back. I wanted to make my apologies and express my gratitude. I wanted to have the opportunity to show Jim that I had changed for good. I wanted to show my parents that I was so grateful for the foundations of faith they had given me in addition to all the love and support along the way. I wanted to make amends and show Jim's parents how grateful I was for their love and support. It was not, nor has it ever been lost on me just how big a role they have played in my sobriety. Had they not been willing to care for Reagan, I would not have gotten the long-term help I needed or been able to reset our lives accordingly. Their unconditional love and support have been paramount, and I am eternally grateful.

Realizations, Reinforcement, and Renewal

I knew I desperately wanted Jim back. But what had changed after Seabrook? Everything. As much as I had wanted to stop in the past, I simply couldn't. More importantly, though, I didn't have the necessary tools to be able to properly manage my fears, resentments, anxieties, failures, insecurities, and cravings. No number of meetings, phone calls, or self-help books would sink in. Not even the countless desperate pleas or even threats from family, regardless of how many and no matter how much of my health was at stake, could have gotten through to my brain before I was completely ready to candidly hear them and accept the truth that I had a problem. Nothing would change until I could completely commit to and be willing to make the changes necessary for myself first and foremost.

Part of the reason it was so awful and shameful to admit to myself, let alone others, that I was an alcoholic is because addiction, especially alcoholism, comes with so many stigmas and preconceived associations. Suggestions of being "that" person closing down the bar every night, or the person in the dark shadows stumbling home late at night, or uneducated, lazy, throwing life away because of growing up in a "bad" home, or frankly just not knowing any better. These are all image issues I struggled with worrying about what people might think of me. What's more, associating a woman with alcoholism might even elicit images of promiscuity. Alcoholism, though, much like depression and mental illness, is not exclusive to any one race, gender, age, or even income level.

Sure, there have been studies done about some of the various correlations, but here I was a well-to-do woman in my twenties from an upper-middle-class home with an Ivy League education, a fully intact family life, breaking the stereotypes and feeling immense shame because of these struggles. How could it even be possible that I could be an alcoholic? It made absolutely no sense at all; I didn't fit the type. Even just the word felt like such a prison to place myself in. When I first said the word "alcoholic," it felt offensive, like an instant judgment because I couldn't find the will to "just stop" whenever I wanted.

What I've learned, though, is that addiction goes beyond the simple fact of overindulging; it is a disease of the body as well as the mind. That seed had taken root so long ago, and I fed it more and more with the poison of indulgence and denial through the years. I was left to my own devices of not holding tight to my own mental health and faith, and I convinced myself that I needed self-medication, and my body and mind then became dependent on it after a while.

I look back now with gratitude and think perhaps I had an easy go of things getting started in the program in that it was basically handed to me, and I didn't need to go looking for it on my own. Well, I couldn't go out and do it on my own, and it was gratefully handed to me (with some forceful encouragement) because I was in too much denial to do it on my own. While it was entirely defeating to be forced to get help and have other people telling me I had a problem that was so bad I needed intervention, I'm grateful my family found help for me.

I'm sure that people with this disease can feel so far gone and out of control that they might not even know where to begin to find the help they desperately need. Sometimes it is an immediate turn-off, the thought of AA, as if there is no way it could possibly be of any use to them, especially considering the stigmas mentioned above.

Perhaps the denial might be so fixed, and some might not be as fortunate as I was to have friends and family who were willing to do all the heavy lifting of finding the facility to provide the help I needed. Help that, despite being forced upon me, I was fortunate to receive and would not be here today without having found it.

For those who do see through the haze and recognize that they have a problem but are too afraid, too ashamed, or simply unwilling to admit it, where are they supposed to turn? It might sound cliché or trite, but if you or someone you know has a problem, the most important thing is to talk to them about it. Providing love and support in every way can be part of the very first step to admitting the problem exists.

For someone who needs help, I recommend AA. It helped me tremendously. Granted, I had the unique and beneficial luxury of having some real veterans of the group walk me through the doors of those first meetings while with the rehab care team. Even so, it was still terrifying to stand up and introduce myself as someone who was an alcoholic. At least I had a group of others with me who were also new to the program, and they were feeling the exact same kind of emotions. Shame, guilt, and awkwardness. But the program has sustained its longevity for a reason—because people support each other.

The program works. Had I not been in a rehab program with veterans and counselors as guides, but still in need of trying to find a meeting all on my own, I could have started at square one and used the amazing resources at AA.org or called the AA helpline to find a meeting or contact info for a local group. Heck, I probably could have gone and talked to the priest at confession or the doctor during one of my checkups and asked for help if I was afraid to talk to a family member because of the shame and guilt I had built up. But the wonderful thing about finding AA meetings online is that if you are a beginner, you can easily find a designated beginners' meeting.

All this to say, if AA is off-putting or sounds scary because of the thought of saying the word "alcoholic" right off the bat, I have yet to encounter a meeting that requires you to speak. My sponsor made sure I knew I should never let fear be a hindrance to walking through the doors and inviting in the help. Everyone else's stories and struggles in those rooms become a network of group support where everyone is pulling for the next person to succeed.

It took one day at a time to start to get my life back, sometimes attending multiple meetings in a day. In the rooms of AA, sitting and talking with others going through the same struggles, I realized I was not alone. I felt like I had become part of a team. We were all working towards the same goal of sobriety and regaining control of each of our lives, and we were rooting each other in the process. It was and continues to be, a wonderful community of love and support, and I would encourage anyone struggling with addiction of any kind to find a meeting and embrace that family. You aren't alone!

It took me having to see the lowest of lows in myself which made me finally willing to take action. I had to feel the hopelessness and unmanageability, the true powerlessness of it all to take action toward a real spiritual change. I was finally able to realize that I could come out of the Seabrook program sorry for my actions without needing to feel ashamed or guilt-ridden. I had to be able to forgive myself so that I could begin to heal.

In AA, they teach you that you do not need to regret the past or wish to shut the door on it. So, if I didn't need to regret the past, things could just go back to normal, right? Definitely not. That door was still ajar and needed to be addressed. Even though I had gone and gotten the much-needed help that all of my family and I wanted, it didn't mean that all was automatically forgiven. I had to take humble care of working through making my amends with my parents, with Jim's parents, and especially with Jim.

The forgiveness of others, though, did come easier than forgiving myself. One of my first counselors said that forgiving yourself is often the hardest part of the healing process. I found that it helped to think of it this way—if God has already forgiven me, then who the heck am I to not forgive myself, too? Yet, it was still the hardest work I had to do, and it was far from over. I still had to prove myself as a changed person, worthy of the love, respect, and trust of those I hurt.

Living in the guilt and shame of the past would only keep me from being able to move forward, leaving the door open for alcoholism to grab me and pull me back down. It took that program at Seabrook and the intense look inward and upward for me to realize that I had been disappointed, angry, and frustrated with myself.

I had felt like making mistakes made ME the mistake. That failing at something made ME a failure. I had not yet learned that a very important distinction exists between an action and a person. It was possible that I did something wrong, but that didn't necessarily make me, Risa, human being, ultimately what is wrong.

Before Seabrook (and this is probably why the drive-thru version of rehab didn't work for me), I had not internalized these distinctions and messages. I still felt like the disease that led me to make so many bad decisions meant I was a mistake and an unlovable person. Once able to internalize the distinction, my guilt and shame have continually been replaced with love, courage, integrity, honesty, hope, faith, and humility. With these, I am also filled with an abundance of gratitude. I learned that instead of trying to be perfect, I could be strong, I could be fearless, I could be me. Perfectly imperfect just as God intended.

I found during my stay at Seabrook as I started to heal that I could let go of the burdens of my imperfections and I discovered that "church" existed outside of the four walls of a building with an altar and a priest. For me, church became any place where I could find the serenity to focus on prayer, reflection, gratitude, and forgiveness. Church could take place while exercising in the morning or watching the sunrise. It could involve finding any quiet space, like a porch swing or a walk through His glorious woods. Anyplace to talk to the God of my understanding to say, *"Thank You."*

Later down the road church would become afternoons looking out at the long-stretched blanket of white, with no sound other than the quietness of snowflakes falling. And long after my mom passed away and we had no headstone, church would be at the beach on a bench overlooking the ocean thinking of loved ones.

I learned to lean on those around me and to thank those who got me through. My Aunt Kate was especially instrumental in helping to find the Seabrook program in the first place, and the inpatient program she found was what fortunately turned our lives around. I was able to thank Jim's parents, and I will be forever thankful for all the support they gave not just to me, but also to Jim, and for helping to take care of Reagan while I was getting help. I was able to humble myself and apologize for the hurt that I know I caused them. And eventually, they were able to forgive me, perhaps cautiously at first, knowing that I still needed to demonstrate that I was a changed woman.

Those divorce papers, though...writing this now, they were filed more than a decade ago! Thank God that Jim had the courage to file them. Every December 7, I look at him and say, *"Thank you for being willing to put the mirror up to my face and having the courage to walk away if that was what it would take!"* And that is exactly what it took. That mirror, seeing myself alone in the mirror, is what helped point me towards sobriety.

Without Jim making what he considers to be the scariest and toughest decision of his life, I wouldn't be here today. These eleven years have unquestionably been taken one grateful day at a time. I know so much more about faith and gratitude after these past eleven years. Gratitude for the big things, sure, but for the small things, also.

Those divorce papers I mentioned could have been filed all the way to completion, and this story would be an entirely different one. Instead, though, Jim and I remarkably and happily just celebrated seventeen years of marriage! And some might say that marriage isn't easy, period, let alone being married to someone with an illness and an unpredictable one at that. Even though I had my first seizure two months before the wedding, little did Jim know what the words "in sickness and in health" would come to mean.

Take his profession out of the equation, as a loving spouse think of how devastating it is to watch and how powerless you can feel when the person you've vowed to love through good and bad, sickness and health, is spiraling out of control with addiction and then struggling with a scary and ongoing illness like epilepsy. When we stood at the altar in 2006, we made those vows, and he has seen me through my failures and fears, the hurt and the losses. The many episodes, traumas, and challenges that each phase of my epilepsy has presented for both of us. And he has stayed.

I am sure there were times when he wished that things were different, easier, or that I hadn't caused him the heartache and worry that I have over the years, but not out of selfishness, more so because he didn't want to see me suffer. That is just the man he is, so compassionate, so giving, so forgiving, and so very loyal to his family. He could have easily given up, seeing how much both my diseases put him through.

There were times, especially after various seizure episodes, and then even more so after surgeries, when Jim needed to be so strong right alongside me, reassuring me (though probably feeling fearful himself) while also picking up the pieces where his teammate could not pull weight any longer.

Talk about a total superdad, managing all the kid schedules; cooking gourmet meals; playing endless rounds of War, Chutes and Ladders, Pop the Pig, and Guess Who?; running laundry; running out for groceries; trying not to run out of patience; and worrying about my possible episodes while also balancing a beyond full-time career in the clinic and operating room.

Sure, we did have help from family, thank goodness, but no one can take the place of Dad or Mom, so while one or two of those tasks may have been alleviated at times, he was taking on so much more than anyone should have ever had to. And that is only one of the many reasons he is the love of my life, my best teammate, and the reason I am still on this wildly ridiculous planet.

At the celebration of our wedding and those sacred vows, during the toasts, a cherished family friend, a Christian Brother, spoke regarding the uniqueness and power of love in a poetic way that touched our hearts. And despite my rerouted brainwaves and all-too-frustrating fuzzy recall, I remember this specific toast so vividly.

As our dear friend Brother Brian attested in his booming voice, "Love is everything. It is the making of dreams and of promises to keep. It is having stars in your eyes and tomorrows in your heart. It is the giving of songs and of silences and the holding of memories only the heart can see. Love can be the sudden magic of a moment or as subtle as a glance from across a room. It can be felt in the soft squeezing of hands, a gentle hug from a child, or the sharing of whispers only two hearts can hear. Without love in our hearts, our lives would be as empty as a tomorrow without a dream."

Jim has been my rock throughout. He was my rock even when he filed for divorce. It was *out* of love that he filed for divorce. It was *because* he loved me so much that he hoped to force me into seeing all that I had to lose if I didn't get help. Yes, I put in the work with the program but only because of his willingness to take a leap of faith that I *would* do it.

To this day, he keeps me on my toes, and we make a better team because he put that mirror up to my face back in 2012. It was love I felt from that subtle glance from across the room, even if it was a hospital room—especially since it was a hospital room. Talk about sickness and health! Those glances were filled with love as we passed the time in the hospital playing Nintendo. It was love when he held me both in my grief after my mother's passing and in the silence of the fear given what was to come with surgery.

In those silences when I couldn't chew, let alone talk, or those playful silences every now when the Phillies are beating the Mets (or vice versa), we still love and enjoy each other. That's what makes our relationship work. We still have fun and have tomorrows in our hearts thanks to the hope and faith that we have in each other.

We also know when the silences are appropriate–as the old wisdom goes, pick your battles! About things big and little, but especially the little things. I've come to understand and appreciate so much about compromise, but that doesn't always have to be a negative thing, as if you are settling.

Compromise to me means working towards a common goal. In our case, or rather, in my case, I can compromise on the need to be super controlling about doing the dishes or struggling to find space in the fridge. On a weekend evening after having put in more than eighty hours of work, having him pour his heart out on the plate cooking us one of his gourmet seafood meals (those are always my favorite!), fridge space and dishes become so petty. Finding unrelenting stacks of Tupperware piling up just doesn't matter when we are both so grateful to be eating together, connecting as a family, and enjoying the delicious food. I can let go of all those frustrations and choose to simply be okay with what is given to me in life, and not struggle so much when things don't go my way.

I could so easily have missed out on the life that I have now with Jim had it not been for his amazingly courageous love. When I saw everything that I stood to lose, I gained an entirely new appreciation for all of him, and we can work with our little missteps and squabbles for what they are–little. I know that I don't always get it right, and we have our moments as any couple does.

But what used to be points of genuine contention are now so much more minimal in comparison. We take care of each other because we are so fortunate to realize how different things could have been (and not for the better) back in 2012. My gratitude and admiration for him as a husband, teammate, father, and physician go beyond words.

I've learned to be grateful for all the people who cross my path and have seen their own storms they've had to weather, as well as weathering mine with me without bailing on me. I am most grateful that I *get* to do all the things a wife and mother does because I was given that opportunity as a second chance.

I thank God often that I didn't accidentally overdose or miss any medications and end up having a life-ending seizure before my sobriety! I was given the gift of continuing my life, a life in sobriety, and I was given a beautiful second chance with my once-in-a-lifetime, one-in-a-million husband, and I am so very grateful.

As it sometimes takes, I had to hit rock bottom to find out just how deep my faith and gratitude were rooted to know that no matter how anxious, chaotic, or even insecure and resentful I might be feeling or how crazy life gets, I can still persevere. Yes, I fell down. Yes, I hit my own personal rock bottom. It might not be ideal or comfortable or fun to fall as hard as we do sometimes, but each time we fall, God is giving us a choice. When you're close to defeat do you rise to your feet or sink in your seat?

By now you have guessed my choice and chosen mantra. "The harder you fall, the higher you bounce." If you really want to get technical about it, the laws of physics say that the height to which an object bounces back up is determined by the amount of potential energy that is converted back into kinetic energy during the collision. But that's neither here nor there. For all the falls and painful impacts, getting back up has made for so much opportunity for growth and new heights instead of sinking lower and lower.

Despite all these opportunities to bounce back up, life has gotten crazy along my journey. Those taps on the shoulder from God are just reminders that I'm not the one driving the bus, that I am not the conductor. I have been plenty insecure at different times in my life about the little things and have seen numerous opportunities to be resentful. But now I have the tools in my toolbox from the program and, more importantly, from having grown a stronger faith in myself and in God's plan. I am equipped to avoid getting derailed and have found a deep gratitude for life!

Changing the Latitude, Improving the Attitude

After staying at Seabrook House, in the summer of 2013, we made the move from New Jersey to Charlottesville, VA where Jim did a one-year fellowship at UVA. We could very easily see that it was by far the best thing for us. We were confident in the wise words of Jimmy Buffet (as alluded to in the heading above), though I, of course, had no thoughts of margaritas anymore.

It was the perfect opportunity to hit that reset button on our relationship with a fresh start and none of my old habits, haunts, or hiding spots anywhere nearby. Moving to a new state, a new part of the country that we were both unfamiliar with was the fresh start we needed. It was as if Seabrook had given me a new beginning altogether, and this move was yet another stepping stone on the journey to change for the better to finally break the cycle of painful and inappropriate choices.

We did not just jump right back into the blissful joy of our relationship as if I had not completely blown it up in the first place. We knew it would take time, and we were working on things step by precious step and enjoying each smile, each time we made each other laugh again. Just before the move, we began meeting with an outstandingly insightful therapist to help with repairing trust and the relationship as a whole.

After the move, we made it a priority to keep meeting with Dr. H (as we so dearly refer to him) via virtual sessions to keep the healing moving in a positive direction. We kept slowly sewing things back together and making sure that the fabric of our lives was appropriately woven together and that we could grow to be an even stronger team than we were before. We are still fortunate enough to utilize Dr. H's help to this day, guiding us and keeping us talking about our relationship, even eleven years after those series of events and seventeen years into our marriage.

Because of the lessons we've learned and all the tools he has given us to keep in our toolbox, we have found a steady ground for our marriage because we would like to avoid a breakdown like before at all costs. And while it was crucial at the time to keep working with Dr. H until things were more secure, we still think it is important to stay on the steady ground and keep meeting with him today. We feel it is imperative to stay communicating and acquiring more tools because that toolbox can never be too full, and we want to keep our road paved and pothole-free for a long time to come.

Thinking about it in different terms, why would you wait until the car has a flat tire and you're stranded on the side of the road to call for a tow truck when you could have been monitoring and checking the air pressure at home the whole time? When we take the time for regular check-ins and are mindful of our circumstances, utilizing our tools and gaining more along the way, we are better able to avoid things that might otherwise grow into immense pitfalls and potholes of heartache.

Once we were in Virginia, the steady progress in our marriage, the repaving of the road, continued. I could see during that time that he was proud of me. I could tell that he saw the faith I had in myself again. In turn, it boosted his own faith and trust in me, and then in us, as well. The road we were repaving was growing stronger in this new phase of our journey.

We were able to rent a small apartment, I got a low-stress part-time job with flexible hours, and Reagan started attending preschool. All the while, and crucial to the success of our continued strengthening of the relationship, I was attending AA meetings regularly and working, *really* working, through the steps of the program to keep myself on track.

Somewhere along the reset of that long and broken but blessed road, Jim began to recognize me as the girl he had fallen in love with. He once again started to see me as the healthy and happy Risa who made him laugh and who was not a source of constant sadness, stress, struggles, pain, or frustration. We were able to finally *get* each other again. I appreciated him on a whole new level, and with the help of our counseling, we found our way back to being an awesome TEAM once again. By the grace of God, I also remained seizure-free for the whole year spent in Virginia.

While I was in the program, I learned that saying the serenity prayer every single day was an essential practice in helping me not only remain sober but also to find peace with accepting the things I could not change, the many things in life that are entirely out of my control. Most especially, I found peace with the fact that my epilepsy itself, even if I was not having episodes on a frequent basis, was unpredictable and out of my control. I learned to keep faith and stay the course. Once Jim started the application and interview process for full-time positions after his fellowship, we were able to begin thinking about and preparing for the next adventure, whatever it would end up being for us.

And my goodness, what an adventure it ended up being! After Jim's fellowship year ended in the summer of

2014, we moved from Virginia to Cooperstown, NY. Talk about another reset. My what a difference in climate! Have you ever had to move your Memorial Day BBQ indoors because of all the frost?

While being home to the iconic Baseball Hall of Fame, Cooperstown is also a quaint but isolated and unique one-streetlight village of only 1,800 year-round residents where it snows ten feet (yes, FEET) annually. It was a bit unsettling at first, realizing we had zero friends or family support to start, but it was another new beginning that we embraced.

I will never forget when Jim interviewed for the job, and I began asking questions about where I was supposed to go shopping. It turns out the answer was simple: that is what the internet is for! I also learned that with small towns like this, whenever something bad happens, or God forbid, your child misbehaves, the entire town will end up knowing all about it! But yes, that quaint and family-friendly small-town characteristic would end up being one of the greatest blessings when I would need it the most.

While I easily established a network of amazing friends through the parents of kids in Reagan's class, it was still a challenge to once again be homebound and all alone with Jim working those long physician hours in the winter months. With such a sacred second chance with Jim and Reagan, however, I refused to waver in being anything other than sober, grateful, and optimistic that we were going to continue to grow and thrive.

I regularly woke up with the thoughts of my sponsor's encouragement to say the serenity prayer (which had become about as routine as breathing) and to always focus on the blessings before bemoaning the burdens and challenges. I utilized the quiet mornings after Reagan left for school to take time to talk to and thank God as I found my church right outside our window. Our property sat on three acres adjacent to a beautiful hops farm of eleven acres.

It was through our window overlooking the expanse of either gorgeous green in summer or white in winter that I got to have my conversations with Him every day in order to maintain sobriety and sanity. It was hard to be anything other than grateful (okay, maybe a little cold) looking at the beauty of His creation, having my family back, and being seizure-free. It was with this newfound gratitude that I found myself thanking people more often, being more open to helping at Reagan's school, and attending more social functions with Jim. I was grateful for the opportunity to do each of these wonderful things.

But, as life sometimes goes, just when I was taking my serenity and peace almost for granted, in October of 2014 (despite still regularly checking with my neurologist and staying on my epilepsy medication), I had a blackout seizure while driving on a major road (well, as major of a road as you can get in Upstate New York) as I was running errands. It becomes clearer and clearer just how true it is that I have angels on my shoulder. That accident was just another tap of God reminding me not to get too cozy in my condition. Praise God, though, that Reagan was not in the car at the time.

Another indicator of divine intervention, it appeared from the scene walk-through that I must have had one of my pre-seizure warning auras and had been in the process of slowing down and pulling over. Thus, I was miraculously able to avoid hurting any other drivers who might have been on the road. After being taken to the hospital via ambulance, I proceeded to have yet another seizure. I recall none of the details, but it was still too close of a call and a life-threatening cause for pause to remind me of life's fragility. I had been actively avoiding all my known triggers, and I had felt fine that morning, otherwise I never would have gotten behind the wheel in the first place.

The worst part of this was how alarming and out of the blue the episode was. It was utterly baffling and frightening to us all, especially since it had come on so suddenly, and I had been taking all my medications. And while the damage to the car rendered it a total loss, we knew it was almost time to replace it soon anyway. Most importantly, we saw that the situation could have turned out so horrifically different, and for that we were beyond grateful.

Unfortunately, though, the State of New York considers any loss of consciousness event as cause for license revocation. With my newfound perspective and perpetual gratitude, I was able to view the crash and fallout from a standpoint that while it may not be ideal to lose my license for almost a full year, by the grace of God, I didn't lose my life, or worse yet, take anyone else's.

The car was gone, and I spent most of 2015 just putting one foot in front of the other. Having been given several opportunities to learn patience, gratitude, faith, and to take things one day at a time, that is exactly what I embraced once again. I took things one day at a time by taking things one step at a time. One faithful step at a time.

The inconveniences of not having a license combined with the recurrence of seizure activity and the instability associated activated the churn of self-pity inside. These stresses and all this self-pity would have been excuses during my previous active addiction to numb myself and my sorrows with alcohol, but in my firm and not-taken-for-granted sobriety, I stayed the course by focusing instead on everything the program taught me. I appreciated the little things, sometimes even that cold weather! Having perspective after my time at Seabrook and the accident, well, it allowed me to appreciate much more of the comfort found in warm hugs from my darling Reagan and enjoying a hot cup of coffee under a cozy blanket.

    I searched for and found those different churches all around me, digging deep into my faith as I continued my work to heal. I enjoyed the serenity and peace of my surroundings. And despite how quickly the snow piled up (and it did amass quite quickly and quite often), I took the opportunity to look out at the blankets of this specific pure white church God put right outside my window, simply repeating the twelve-step prayers and mantras that Wendy, my sponsor, had taught me over the years as she helped me in my journey to remain sober. Each day was just that, a brand-new day, and on those days that may not have been going so well, I reminded myself of my mom's old saying, "Have your little pity party and move on."

    Although I felt inconvenienced and discouraged being unable to drive at times, I didn't wallow in my sorrows with so many other good things to see around me. I soaked up every smile my daughter provided because I knew just how quickly she might end up gone if I were to slip into my old habits. I thought about and acknowledged how far I'd come and cherished the gift of another chance with my family. I took the time to journal about my program step-work and simply lived each day as it came. I trusted that I was on the path (albeit not driving) God intended. Our road was repaved, potholes always getting repaired, and now we got a bit of snow cover, and we were still feeling so very blessed.

    Having a five-year-old with a surprisingly packed social and extracurricular calendar and a husband whose hospital hours were hectic, being without a car and a driver, I was certainly left with one arm tied behind my back. But as the motto goes, "Don't freak out, we'll figure it out!" And that's just what I did, one day, one activity at a time. It required a lot of creative and sometimes pricey online shopping. It required having the determination and mindset each day to say, "I *will* figure out a way to manage this puzzle of errands, school carpools and drop-offs, and extracurriculars." All the while staying centered by attending my own personal church for serenity each snowy morning.

As the year unfolded after the accident, Reagan had a lot of questions and understandable fears surrounding my health since this was somewhat of a new revelation about how unpredictable my condition could be. She had previously been a little too young to fully understand all the complexities of my epilepsy, but this episode made her very frightened given that I needed to be hospitalized, our car was totaled, and I could no longer do my usual driving anymore. Heck, she had never even witnessed one of my seizures that she could remember before that one. This was life-altering, and she was still so young.

Reagan's own brain tended to rush right to the worst-case scenarios, so the key to managing this new chaos thrown into her world was, and continues to be, empowering her with more information. More transparency brings to light things she may have been fearing the most, making them a little less scary. As the old saying goes, "Knowledge is power." The more she knows about my condition, the history, what triggers my seizures, what they look like, and what medications I take and why—the better able she is to manage.

Giving her as much knowledge as possible removed certain elements of the "fear of the unknown" behind my condition but certainly not all of it, and it did nothing to change the unpredictability of it. While she had a few worries about those worst-case scenarios, we could at least give her the best-case scenarios and acknowledge the true uncertainty of the more likely scenarios that existed in between.

We told her as much as we could at an age-appropriate level, leaving at the basic nature of "Mommy's got a brain that works a little funny sometimes, but the doctors know how to help with different medications to keep things working properly."

At one point, I was able to come up with the image of an electrical outlet or fuse box at home to help her understand things. I explained how sometimes at home we blow a fuse for one of the outlets and she sees Daddy go to the breaker box to reset it to get things working properly again. The house never burns down, and while the power might go out momentarily, nothing catastrophic happens.

In explaining things this way, we showed her that my brain may short-circuit occasionally, but I am going to survive and be okay. Sometimes my brain just blows a fuse and needs to be reset—that's why I take the medicine! Being able to use such an image to connect the episode to something familiar and fixable was essential.

Now, while that episode of 2014 brought the issue to light for her, we told her this was an unusual occurrence seeing as things had been so calm for so long. We assured her that she didn't need to worry about things happening like that all the time. Most importantly, we made sure she understood that despite now having suddenly comprehended that her mom has a brain disease, it didn't change who I was to her. I was still the same mom who loved her, who cooked and cleaned, who snuggled and read to her and prayed with her every day. And, as time went on, and she was living with me having epilepsy, we would manage her fears as they would arise, with openness and honesty.

The biggest complications came from having her life and routine upended when I was not able to drive anymore. But much like my own day-to-day challenges, one step at a time in our new routine, I reminded her that it was not her job to worry about how to figure out her schedule. She still had Daddy for support, and we could trust and thank God that this was a seemingly isolated incident. I asked her to have the same faith and trust as I did, that the doctors would figure out the wiring of Mommy's brain and rectify these rare glitches once and for all.

We absolutely wanted Reagan to understand that this was something we had dealt with before and could manage again. We continually made sure she knew that I loved her, that her daddy loved her, and that I was not going anywhere. Once she had that in her heart and mind, and she was more aware and mindful of my condition, I could see how she was paying more attention to how I was feeling, acting, and reacting to different things, especially given the struggles surrounding life without a car.

As a teenager now, though, she doesn't recall 2014 being a time of worry or recall the reality of my epilepsy sinking in. As her various fears arose at the time, we managed them as they came, and it seems we did a good job considering she doesn't remember being afraid! This was my first opportunity to show her that life isn't all about how hard you can hit the fastball straight down the middle (though that is a wonderful feeling). Instead, it is about how you can adjust your swing to the curveball that life and God throw at you.

It was a wonderful chance as her mom and role model to show that every morning is a choice to either get up or give up. Every morning was my opportunity to show her that I was choosing faith and gratitude for our life with all the challenging circumstances swirling around us instead of staying in bed (albeit so warm and cozy) and wallowing or worrying. Sure, she expressed her own worries, but I prayed with her and made it a point to reassure her on an annoyingly frequent basis that I was feeling healthy. We made it a practice to look on the bright side of circumstances, and we both made great friends in the area who provided support and became essential helpers in our times of need.

The 2014 episode, though, and any of the especially unexpected ones, could have easily led me to feel knocked down physically, emotionally, and even spiritually. Naturally, I did have my moments of going through the pain, anger, the lows of feeling knocked down. But, as has been said by many, it is not the number of times you get knocked down but whether you still choose to get back up.

To persevere, to get back up and keep the faith, and to not give up is what it means to be a true fighter. In the first chapter of the Book of James, James states so beautifully that we should always "consider it pure joy... whenever [we] face trials of many kinds because [we] know that the testing of [our] faith produces perseverance" (James 1:2-3). We can't just improve without being tested. It is through testing that we get the opportunity to choose to grow.

It is this faith, this genuine character- and fortitude-testing journey, that I trained my whole life for. Much like a runner will train for a marathon and learn to persevere through the pain and the discomfort, I have trained for this with each test that has come my way, and I would need endurance as more curveballs would come my way further in my race. I have practiced and learned the music to play in that beautiful eternal symphony.

I have continued practicing, learning, relearning, and getting back up despite all the curveballs, intermissions, tempo changes, and wildly difficult challenges that have come my way with this unpredictable and mind-boggling disease. That is how you approach a life of difficulty and pain, never giving up hope and never ceasing in the belief that God has got you, no matter how long the road may stretch before you.

Even with the big accident of 2014, I was so very grateful for a clear head, for having my life back, and for all those who were supporting and loving me throughout. I was able to earnestly thank God for my parents' support, for Jim's parents' support, and for their forgiveness and grace in allowing us to focus on the bright future ahead instead of dwelling on my past mistakes.

I regularly thanked (and still do thank) God (and Jim) every seventh of the month for the courage in making that potentially marriage-ending decision, and for bringing me, and us, back to life on the broken, then repaved (and then becoming often snow-covered) road. We lived through 2014 and 2015 with perseverance, but I couldn't do it alone.

By that point, my parents had become full-time snowbirds and would spend winters in Florida, so no amount of amazing grandchild cuteness could be enough to bribe them to spend time with us during a bloody cold winter visit. It would have been easy to ask them for help. Heck, I wouldn't have even needed to ask because they would have just done it without me asking, if only it'd just been warmer!

Losing my license and living in a one-streetlight town, beautiful as it is, is an amazing place to see the gorgeous and colorful months of fall with a temperate couple of summer weeks on the lake. And, of course, I think I've mentioned the snow. Beautiful, indeed, but it all put me in a position where I didn't have any other choice but to ask for help from others. We were no longer living in an urban area that made transportation easy. Uber and DoorDash were simply not options at the time, so I was brought to humility in having to ask for help from friends I made through places like Reagan's school.

In that respect, I needed to put my pride aside and ask for support, especially when in those moments freaking out over the puzzle of managing schedules and groceries. Instead of feeling sorry for myself or embarrassed about needing help or drinking to cover my fears about such insecurities, I had faith, and I counted every single blessing.

I *got* to ask for help with Reagan's transportation and groceries for the family. Just a year prior we could have been working out shared custody details and weekend visitation across states, but here I was managing how to get help for a grocery run for the whole family. I was sober, I had a little girl who looked up to me and a husband laughing with me again, and I was beyond thankful to *get* to beg for help from all the people who came to my aid.

And while they might not have been able to save my brain entirely, my helpers saved my sanity during that time when I was humble enough to ask for help. Sometimes they showed a beautiful willingness to help even when I didn't ask because they saw how difficult it was for a prideful and independent person like me to be able to ask for help, thinking of it as a sign of weakness. When people would generously offer to help, I gladly accepted it. In addition to help with errands, I sometimes asked these friends to come over just so that I wouldn't be alone and afraid of the unknown. I got help with anything and everything possible.

My life was full of angels on earth providing me with assistance and assurances, rallying by my side, and giving me vital help during those stressful times of managing schedules and logistics. While a slight medication change seemed to help me maintain stability, I believe the support from those friends keeping my stress levels down is what enabled me to remain seizure-free for all of 2015.

Freezing Toes, New Baby Clothes

For as long as we could remember, Jim and I had always hoped to give Reagan a sibling, but my seizures and addiction had caused a significant derailing of those efforts. After more than two years since our reunification, with my seizures well in control, and having put so much work into repairing our marriage, we felt that we were honestly and completely back together again, an indivisible team, so Jim and I tried working a little harder at giving Reagan a sibling. There was zero luck at first, probably due to my polycystic ovaries. So, we decided it was time to seek a referral for a fertility specialist in Albany.

Once I was able to get my license back, it was easier to make those long treks to Albany to see the specialist, and though it had been quite a long shot in the first place, our second amazing miracle baby, Julia Kathryn, was born in November of 2016 just four days after Jim and I celebrated our tenth wedding anniversary, an incredible milestone most definitely to be cherished, considering how close we'd come to separating not four years prior! And honestly, she was such a miracle considering all the ups and especially the downs of the previous six and a half years!

I had been genuinely one drink away from divorce, and yet here we were, a full family of FOUR! I looked upward and inward and realized I needed to hit that rock bottom just to be able to experience the sheer joy of this little miracle baby girl who finally completed our family. She really had been heaven-sent and worth every step of the journey that God had sent us on to bring her into our world. As the fairy godmother from Cinderella so wisely proclaimed, "Even miracles take a little time." Reagan was beyond excited at the fun of being a doting big sister. My heart was so full, it felt like our family had been missing something for so long, and it was finally complete!

Family complete? Check. Brain working? Check…ing on it. Unfortunately, my brain was still not exactly as I thought it should be. Despite enjoying and cherishing the calm of 2017 with our new blessing in Julia, 2018 kicked off with what would be the first of almost weekly auras/partial seizures and some seizures that ended up being awful with post-episode delusions (among those, delusions of alien abductions). After my car accident and seizure in 2014 and the uptick in activity since then, the doctors were forced to take a deeper look into the underlying causes of my epilepsy.

By this point, Reagan was eight and was beginning to be a firsthand witness to these episodes, and for someone of her age, that can be scary and unpredictable. It was at this age, too, that she can recall it settling in, the realization that I wasn't quite as normal as the other healthy people. People who didn't have to take nine pills each day. Despite telling her that I was taking my medicine and seeing doctors like I was supposed to, she still couldn't quite understand why I kept having to go to the hospital.

She wasn't displaying alarm at having to be home with me alone in case anything happened, but we still felt it important that she knew what to do if anything did happen. Having to teach your kids how to dial 911 in the event of an emergency is important for any family, but I feared that one day she might have to do it for real because I was having an episode.

Again, since knowledge is power, we made sure she knew what signs to look out for in case I was having an episode, but we also reassured her all the while that we were taking all the necessary steps to keep day-to-day life as normal as possible. That doesn't mean she didn't still have questions about why the episodes kept happening or what we could do to make things better. Thankfully, my amazing child never displayed stress at such a level that her grades or behavior suffered (she really is amazing).

Often, after the episodes, I would ask if she needed anything from me to help her through it, and sometimes all she needed was a simple hug. Sometimes we would say a prayer together which assured her that I had faith that I was going to be okay and reminded her that she could talk to God whenever she was scared, too. I told her she could also try to journal, so her thoughts and feelings didn't get bottled up, since it is a great way to get things out.

We had prayed the accident would be a one-off, and at first it had seemed so since I was able to get my license back and remain seizure-free throughout my pregnancy. However, once my pesky brain continued to act up, we finally felt the need to revisit the option the doctors had mentioned what felt like a lifetime ago: brain surgery. We knew I wouldn't be getting better by continuing to roll the dice each time with different medications, and that if a possible (albeit terrifying!) solution existed, we should at least explore it. The doctors laid out a two-fold process.

It wasn't as simple as reviewing yet another MRI and saying, "Yep, that's the spot that needs to come out!" Hey, if it had been that easy all along, I would have spared myself and everyone else all the stress and heartache from the get-go. No, they told me that my type of temporal mesial sclerosis of the right frontal lobe needed to be treated very carefully so as to not lose any critical function. Definitely on board in that respect! And they would need even fancier MRIs to make sure that the lesion seen back in 2008 was the only seizure source.

They needed to see if any other problem areas existed, basically. I would need to do neuropsychiatric testing to make sure I wouldn't lose function by removing that lesion (in addition to anything else they may come to find), and it would be an intense process that could span years, draining me mentally and physically.

Now, when it came time to be honest with the girls about what the different brain surgeries involved, Jim and I found it key to not only empower both the girls with as many facts as we could but also manage their expectations surrounding possible outcomes as well as the difficulties that could arise from a recovery standpoint. They needed to reach the realization that coming out of the hospital, I wasn't going to walk in the door and get right back to all the usual supermom stuff that I was used to doing. What we found is, and this goes for most things in parenting with this type of condition, we must be honest about things that are horribly but unmistakably true.

If we had decided to tiptoe around the fact that my seizures were happening at a greater frequency, that wasn't going to do them any good when it was clear that they were worried and could see the truth firsthand. Ahem, it's called an elephant in the room! Pretending the bad things aren't true doesn't make them go away or make them any less terrifying.

Talking through the biggest fears, walking through all the available information, and providing the girls with our best guess at the true uncertainties of the situation was a start. Telling them that I felt good going into the surgery and that I had remarkable confidence in the doctors made them feel a little less frightened. And being honest about not knowing exactly what the future may hold, but that we had faith, was more transparent and better than just pretending as if none of this scary stuff was happening at all. Empty assurances would not serve them well in the long run.

One of the lessons my parents passed along to me, and quite importantly so, was that as a child (and then even sometimes still as an adult) it was okay to feel my feelings, especially during dark times of struggle, sadness, and stress.

I needed to be able to feel my feelings to be able to better process them before reacting or immediately sinking into those feelings and letting them define me or determine the next steps I took in haste. The feeling of anger shouldn't necessarily be ignored—but anger when manifested towards others is not healthy. Anger that leads to a cool, calm, and collected discussion about how to resolve the conflict that led up to what caused the anger in the first place—that is the goal of engaging anger.

So, then, take the time to feel your feelings and process them, and then you will be able to dive in and discuss them in detail and get to the root of those feelings. But if you choose to deny your feelings, especially if you choose to deny the feelings of a child by telling them "Don't be ____," well, that is simply nonsense. *Don't be scared, don't be silly, don't be sad, don't be upset.* You might as well be telling them not to be themselves.

By that same token, telling Reagan, "Don't be scared," was futile. But affirming her feelings by saying that we understood her fear, we could then offer some insight as to how she could calm herself down and make herself less fearful. Showing her the things she had the ability to control can provide comfort in knowing what to expect.

Then, of course, because kids do thrive on routine, we continued to keep everything as routine as possible during this time, including all activities, bedtimes, and family dinners when

Jim wasn't on call. When my episodes became more frequent, however, it became clearer that I was going to need to prepare her for the possibility of something drastic. So, for this, we told her that I was going to have some special pictures taken of my head to see if the doctors could fix the circuit breaker in my brain so that it worked a little better.

The steadiness of that routine, coupled with trying to make fun memories would hopefully be enough to outweigh the stressful ones (apple picking in the fall, sledding our awesome steep hill of a backyard in winter, trips to the museums in Rochester during my consultations, etc.). The goal was for them to remember the fun of these happy family outings instead of nonstop talk of stress, seizures, and surgery.

We did our best to continue keeping communication open so that all questions she might have got answered, and we made sure to let her know what to expect with all the next steps so that she was always aware of what was happening, that was all she needed. Well, that and consistent love from both of us. We poured out so much love all over her because, as the episodes increased, I knew that I was facing a trial, and not just for me, but for the whole family, and love sees all things through.

After several more MRIs, it was decided that I would need to undergo some intense monitoring of my brain in Rochester, and they scheduled intracranial brain surgery to place wires directly onto my four lobes for seizure monitoring during the summer of 2019. Though the fear and stress about them cutting open my head and what might be revealed was very present, we chose to focus on the blessings amongst us. Our girls. Our home. Each other! I was like Dory from *Finding Nemo*; I found myself set up with a goal, motivated, and woke up each morning, determined to just keep swimming.

Having had to try so many medications since the initial discovery of the lesion that they proposed to remove back in

2008, we knew this could eventually be a possibility, and now it was finally time to face the music and move forward with the temporal lobe resective surgery. With our two precious girls to be considered, it just felt like it was the right time to take the invasive steps to work towards seizure freedom by whatever means necessary.

As had become usual, I looked inward and upward. After all, you never know how strong you are until strong is truly your only choice. In this case, we realized that it was time, and I had no choice but to be strong—and I had that sturdy Irish Catholic strength that was modeled for me with my amazing female lineage working in my favor!

Once we'd finally decided to move towards inpatient monitoring, we prepared Reagan with an arsenal of information, and we were blessed with tons of support from our amazing family. Each time we had to make any decisions, we made sure she understood what was happening and what the timeline would look like. The biggest thing we had to prepare her for (other than my having to be gone for a week) was that my head was going to be shaved. That was what seemed to upset her the most. Having me in the hospital also ended up causing more questions, but we always made sure to focus on the good that was going to come from everything happening in this process.

Once the medications weren't really doing a great job of keeping my seizures under control, the procedure was the best chance for the doctors to get an opportunity to find out where my tripped fuse was located and then see if we could get that breaker fixed for good! At the time, Julia was still far too young to grasp any of the big picture of what was going on, so we just kept telling her that Mommy and Daddy loved her, and Mommy just needed to see special doctors to get everything fixed and would be back very soon.

The ever-smiley and open-armed darling that she was (and still is), she didn't realize what I meant by needing a haircut until after seeing the full buzzcut after the surgery. She wasn't a fan of it or the headscarf that I wore. In fact, she tried to yank it off a couple of times, but I think the shorter hair was even more upsetting. A Phillies hat with fake hair underneath didn't seem to upset her, though! You really can find anything on the internet.

Most importantly, we made sure that we just kept loving the heck out of them and focusing on all the fun things to do that whole summer instead of spending much time letting worry or anxiety make us scared or upset. No one wanted Mommy in the hospital (probably most especially me), so I just kept reminding the girls that hair grows back, and that I had enough faith that this would all lead to the wonderful freedom from seizures we had been praying for all along!

As August of 2019 rolled around, I had my first surgery—intracranial seizure monitoring—at the University of Rochester Medical Center. First, the doctors and nurses gave me another fancy haircut...and by that, I mean they shaved my entire head. But hair grows back, and it would later give me a new lens through which I would view the concept of a bad hair day.

Next, they cut two hook-like incisions in the top of my head where they inserted wires to directly attach to my brain. The girls were both incredibly remarkable. They were taken aback a little by the haircut and by my newly bandaged head, but they were so spoiled while I was in the hospital, and I still got to send them my love from the hospital bed via FaceTime when possible.

I would send people pictures of the surgical scars from this surgery and say that it was from my "horn removal" surgery. I figured that if I could joke about my situation, and even laugh at myself with a lighthearted attitude, it would permit others to do so as well. In addition to strength, my Irish Catholic family gave me quite a wicked sense of humor.

After the "horn removal," the doctors tapered me off of my medications in order to monitor the full activity of my brain and map out where exactly the seizures were generating. determine what part of my brain would be coming out in the surgery, and if I would be losing any important functions. I had to push a button any time I felt a seizure coming on or had any "funny" feelings. It was brutal; it was also painfully scary just waiting for what felt like the inevitable.

Jim stayed by my side the entire time and helped pass the time by watching some of our favorite silly shows and playing some quality games on the Nintendo. He made me feel safe because at any moment one of those dreaded seizures could kick in since my meds were being tapered down. He made sure all my hook-ups and monitors were working properly and that the nursing staff and doctors were taking good care of me. He was definitely a blessing to have at the bedside as both caring husband, and a medical professional.

There were still times when I'd ask, "Why me?" but then I remembered to flip that coin over and instead think the question, "Why not?" I can handle it, and it could be so much worse. I have a family, I have love, and I have access to amazing medical care. I have a deep faith, so why *not* me? If anyone in my house or my family must undergo this kind of wild uncertainty, stress, character testing, and character-building procedure, I would rather it be me than one of my still young, though brave and darling, children.

God had set me on this journey years before and had blessed me with what may have been trials at the time, but had also given me all the tools, insight, and wisdom to know when to put down the pen, and the strength to be able to endure a hardship like this, and so it only makes sense that this would be part of my journey.

Faith Over Fear

It was around this time that I embraced the motto of "faith over fear" because I firmly believed that I would get through all the hurdles and setbacks brought on by my condition. As I had learned through the years, God would be present and continue showing me the way. I learned to walk by faith after having achieved steady sobriety, one step, one day, one hour, and sometimes even just one deep breath at a time. I can say with certainty that the power of positive thinking as well as the incredible power of prayer is what held me up and got me through each of these trying times.

Positivity, to me, meant being able to find joy in the little things from each day, the baseball games that were on (Go Phillies!), the delicious milkshakes Jim would bring home, and the joy of envisioning myself living to the fullest again and taking advantage of every single day instead of fearing what might happen. Much like the dominos of negative thinking that can fall and make you feel worn out and flattened, the power that comes from positive thinking, at least for me, has had a domino effect, but in an uplifting manner that is not only beneficial mentally but physically as well. And, let's face it, being positive tends to make others want to look on the bright side as well! It can work for exponential good all the way around if you prepare for a possible storm while enjoying the sun as it shines, not focusing on the worst-case scenarios.

Based on the results of the monitoring, as well as the additional neuropsychological and functional testing, it was determined that the lesion could be safely removed and that was seen as the most likely option to create a "cure" and give me the best chance of being completely seizure-free. There was even a bit of hope that I could eventually get to taper down off my medications as well. The temporal lobe resective surgery was then scheduled for January of 2020.

I learned that there is a reason for the expression, "It's as easy as brain surgery." Talk about an opening for fear! I was not exactly excited about the procedure. I wasn't resentful either, though. I knew this needed to happen, and I was grateful we had this plan. I had an opportunity to achieve seizure freedom! All that testing (not just medical, but character-testing, as well) would not have been in vain.

I kept my eyes on the prize, I listened to the doctors, and I knew it was necessary. I couldn't go over it. Couldn't go under it. I just had to go through it, and I would come out stronger. I knew that with Jim by my side, we could absolutely handle this! It was going to take a team of helpers and an army of prayer warriors in my corner, family and friends, and really the entire greater Philadelphia chapter of the Sisters of Mercy.

And then I got hit by a pitch that knocked the wind of certainty out of me, and my world came crashing down just before surgery. My mom's health had begun to gradually fall apart. Since our time in Cooperstown, her rheumatoid arthritis had weakened her immune system and made her more susceptible to infection. Because of this, she contracted a rare lung disorder, and throughout all of 2018 and 2019, her overall health quickly and steadily declined. It was devastating to see her lose the ability to walk on her favorite beaches and play with her grandkids. As we each battled our own afflictions, we relied on our faith, strength, sense of humor, and loved ones to help us through. She continued her work as an associate with the sisters for as long as she could, she prayed for me, and she prayed *with* me, until right before my surgery. She displayed the strength of a true warrior.

One of my absolute fondest memories from her final months was from right before my first surgery when we got to have a dream come true of a meet-and-greet with our favorite Phillies players. My dad set up the whole thing through a Phillies Charities auction. Along with Jim and the girls, my mom, my dad, and I got to meet and talk to some of the best players right on the Citizen's Bank Park field.

We got to meet Scott Kingery, Mikael Franco, and the always-incredible Mike Schmidt! Mom was just being Mom when, in her wheelchair, as Hector Neris was leaning in to say hello, she shouted, "Move outta the way–there's Kruk!" (she could be a bit bossy and hilarious). Seeing my mom laughing so hard with John Kruk and embracing Mike Schmidt was one of the most priceless moments that I will always cherish.

Mom passed away the Sunday before my Thursday brain surgery. She told me to be strong and that I did not need to be afraid—she would be watching over me. At that point, I still had a choice. I could be resentful and angry, sad and depressed, all of which I experienced in waves, of course. Or I could focus on my gratitude. I was so grateful that my mom was finally out of pain. When I take a step back and consider the timing, as well, I am grateful. It was January of 2020 when the pandemic first hit. She was suffering from a terminal lung condition, and with a respiratory virus like COVID-19 going around, she very likely would not have survived.

I was obviously sad that she had to leave this physical world and all of us so soon, and I have missed her every single day since then, but she promised to watch over us and send us rainbows from above. I took comfort, though, in realizing that she probably asked God to be taken at that exact time so that she could be the lead angel conducting an immeasurable chorus of angels as I was about to undergo my procedure. All that gratitude and faith prevented me from falling off what could have been an obvious and disastrous cliff of self-doubt, fear, and sorrow. Of course, I had my moments of wandering back into the negatives, the sorrow, and the self-pity, but I knew Mom wouldn't want me to get stuck in that gloom. And if my path did start to head towards darkness, I would look around for light and for those rainbows she promised me.

I am always a little emotional and yet exhilarated each time ReRe follows through on her promise, because send lovely rainbows she certainly does! Sometimes when we haven't even had a storm, we still get beautiful rainbows shining as bright as heaven could produce! That is why I know she is most definitely keeping her promise. To guide us, and in some cases, to protect us. Just to let us know that, indeed, she is still with us in some way. Just as Jesus told his closest friends in Matthew 28:30 that He would be with them even until "the end of the age," so I see ReRe live on, with my children's sass and spunk that they inherited from her (and from me), and even more so in the kindness, compassion, and perceptiveness they show to all.

Whenever we do see those rainbows she sends us, we all look and point, calling it another ReRe Rainbow! We use it as an opportunity to say hello to her once again because we know she is visiting us. I have a whole room in our house of rainbow photos taken when she has come for those special visits, and we call it the ReRe Rainbow Room. I have found that it is a place of significant peace, comfort, prayer, and reflection, getting to be there with Mom.

Before the surgery, I let the tears out whenever they came, but I kept focusing on the fear and the anger—and staying in those places of emotional fear and anger took up too much energy and ended up eating me up on the inside. I found that when I take the time to focus on God's strength and actually make it a point to flex my faith, when instead of being afraid or angry, I choose to show my love and gratitude, that is when I become less fearful and less focused on the pain and anger this situation causes or how much worse it could be. God's strength, and my faith, love, and gratitude—these are all things that have been modeled for me through my parents and several amazing female role models throughout my life.

My mother, my godmother who has since passed away after a beautifully courageous battle with breast cancer, my grandmother who lost her battle with pancreatic cancer (all while letting her joy and laughter be what we all remember about her), my mother's three sisters (all of whom are like mothers to me)…the strength of independent Irish Catholic women is unparalleled, and I learned from some of the absolute best. My mother and her sisters were inducted into the Hall of Fame at their high school; that is how marvelously successful they all are.

I love and admire each of them for the dedication they each put into their lives, their educations, their professions, and their families. They boldly paved the way for other women in their fields, and I am so proud that my girls have had such loving, smart, and fun ladies in their lives to look up to and who they can lean on as I have gotten to do for my entire life. The humor that they taught me was, at times, what sustained me in my darkest moments. And my girls get that gift, as well.

Operation: Fix Risa's Brain

The surgery took about five hours. This time, I was fortunate enough that they only shaved half my head, which I couldn't help but laugh at. I think my hair is forever growing at different lengths now, and I am okay with that because at least it is still on my head...for now. Until the girls start dating, that is, because then I'm sure I'll probably be tearing it out. The scar looks like something out of the movie *The Matrix*. It took over one hundred stitches to close the Y-shaped wound. The recovery hurt more than any other physical pain I have ever experienced in my entire life.

It was painful just to blink, to chew, or even to try talking. Let's just say, also, that Jim has lost all right to complain about headaches ever again! He certainly isn't going to get any sympathy from me, anyway. The headache was excruciating. Imagine the atomic bomb of all migraines. Only worse. It hurt to even blink. But I kept reminding myself that it was only temporary. I kept remembering what my mom had gone through in her final months and how strong she had been. I knew that I had it in me to be that strong, too, to honor her. Who was I to complain, anyway? This is nothing compared to the pain I saw her go through towards the end. This is just a tiny little blip on the scale of what God went through on the cross to save me.

The strength of my mom inspired me to keep pushing forward, moment by moment, bite by bite, and chew by painful chew. My entire mindset shifted about a lot of things after that climb—after what could have been a life-ending or, at the very least, debilitating procedure. If anything had gone even the slightest bit wrong by even a millimeter while they were poking around in my brain, it could have been the end of me or, at the very least, the end of me as I knew myself to be. It has been a constant battle having to give up or, at the very least, let go of those memories that I so desperately wish I could still have. I feel so grateful, though, that I remember the beautiful strength of ReRe and how she has been a consistent inspiration to me to keep pushing ahead.

I was able to start seeing my priorities from a completely different perspective with an entirely new appreciation for my life, as challenging as it might have been. What were once awful and big problems were not so big anymore. The view from the top of the metaphorical Everest of this journey made everything else seem so small. Brain surgery forced me into a mindset of looking at even the most stressful of tasks (paying bills, breaking up children's fighting, fixing major home repairs, etc.) through a lens of *get to* vs. *got to* (or *have to*). When I realized that I *get* to do each task as a gift, my heart was lighter and the blessings all around me became clearer!

I so desperately wish I had more stories or quotes to expand upon how funny, amazing, "firm-yet-fair," and inspirational my mom was. I wish I could recount how particular vacation memories will stick with me forever or how an awesome thing happened this one time during a summer beach trip with the family, and I will never stop laughing about it. Unfortunately, the truth is that this epilepsy and the brain surgery have robbed me of the ability to recall far too many of these types of precious memories. It has even caused me to struggle with mid-short-term memory issues, as well.

Truthfully, my struggles to remember where I last put my phone or keys are probably not entirely uncommon, especially given my age now, but it becomes even more frustrating when compounded with the long-term consequences of epilepsy. The doctors have told me that each seizure did a little more damage to the neurons and that as part of the surgery, there are certain "pathways" that have been cut off. Kind of like when Google Maps reroutes you if you make a wrong turn, my brain is simply unable to adjust quickly and may never be able to recall some of those connections like it once did.

The doctors also explained, in somewhat technical terms, that my brain acts somewhat like a hard drive. The files have been saved there, but my brain doesn't know which folder I put the memory in and can't quite access it because the folder or link has been broken or the name has been changed and can't be located. It is quite a complex and fascinating organ, the brain. A genuinely amazing muscle, not to mention critical to all functioning. Seeing as it is so incredibly complex, when there's any damage inside and it doesn't work properly, it is remarkably difficult to repair!

Whenever I hear someone start a conversation with something like, "Oh! Do you remember that one time when...?" I cringe with discouragement even before hearing the rest of the sentence. Often, I simply don't remember whatever event they are asking about. If they show me a picture, sometimes my brain may be able to connect the dots and find the pathway to pull that file from the dusty corner of my brain, but it breaks my heart that I do not have so many more hilarious ReRe stories (like when she asked which aisle she could find lemon zest in at the grocery store...or how she once accidentally seasoned over a hundred deviled eggs with cinnamon instead of paprika). I wish I could share more stories with my girls of vacations, sporting events, or details from milestone birthdays, but that's not how my brain works anymore, unfortunately.

I don't need any specific ReRe stories to remember who she was to me and how much of her love and legacy still live in me. And I do remember how much of a champion she was on my behalf. She was my biggest cheerleader on the sidelines of almost every single one of my softball games, even if she was terrified of watching me get hit by pitches and sliding into second base on my face, or even taking fastballs to the chest behind home plate as a catcher. "Way to go, Mo!" she'd always yell, despite her utter distaste for the nickname. "I did *not* name you after one of the Three Stooges, my dear!" She stood up for me when my coaches didn't think I could excel at academics and athletics at the same time. This "nerd" proved them wrong! Unfortunately, this nerd can't remember the same formulas and equations she once used to.

I think it is common for people who have had seizures or some sort of brain trauma or surgery to experience these issues. What feels even more maddening is that I cry about not being able to remember really important things that I wish I could share with the girls to tell them later in life, and yet I have no problem reciting ridiculous lyrics at the drop of a dime (here's looking at you, Sir Mix-A-Lot and your timeless gem, "Baby Got Back"). I still remember every essential from the Motown catalogue of hits. These memory issues are challenging, they are annoying, and sometimes they even cause great sadness. But then I realize that so many people have it so much worse than me.

For instance, those who suffer from Alzheimer's, ALS, or other degenerative diseases, experience significantly more suffering than I have. Then I think also about the caregivers who feel helpless as they watch those in their care slowly getting worse, who feel robbed of the ones they love. Sure, my memory issues are very difficult at times, but I am functioning—and what is even more, the doctors have been able to treat me for my seizures!

Not only that, tools do exist to help people like me. My most recent and incredibly diligent neurologist, Dr. Ganguly, recommended in particular, an online program called Hobscotch (which stands for **Ho**me-**B**ased **S**elf-Management and **C**ognitive **T**raining **Ch**anges Lives). It was developed by the epilepsy center and utilizes the help of a cognitive coach and psychological strategies to enhance memory function through various modules and "training" sessions. I just started the modules but have already found it beneficial and recommend it to others with epilepsy suffering from the same memory frustrations.

So, even if it takes some pathway re-routing, the regular use of Google Maps, diving into all the photos and journaling my hands can manage, and tools like HOBSCOTCH, I will do whatever it takes so that going forward, I can try and experience my memories through words and pictures. My struggles are so minor in comparison, and even though they feel like an uphill mountain to battle up, I'll be singing with joy the whole way up!

A Brand-New Outlook

Things just seemed to make more sense after the surgery, in all ways. It gave me a whole different perspective on a lot of things in life, both big and small. And managing minor crises or inconveniences wasn't such a hassle or a bother anymore. If one of the girls forgot an errant lunch or homework assignment at home and I was called upon to bring it to the school at the last minute during an already otherwise hectic day with subzero temperatures and snow falling like crazy, I didn't think to myself, *COME ON!! Do I really HAVE to?!*

I'd already climbed my metaphorical Everest and gone through so many blockades in my path, I learned to be more than okay with bringing my blessed children whatever they needed. Food that we could afford, in a car that had gas that we also could afford on roads that were beautifully plowed, with a driver's license I had finally gotten back after my incident. Breaking up those delightful sisterly squabbles didn't seem like as much of an issue when it provided me an opportunity to remind these beautiful kids to be kind to one another a hundred times a day because they are playing with and learning valuable lessons from each other in a safe neighborhood and not out on the streets in gang wars. These are all amazing gifts that I *get* to do and not upsetting things I *have* to do.

When Jim is gone because he is on call, it is because he's *got* a job. And what is even more amazing, he's a healer. He's needed at the hospital, but he will always return after his shift. I think about military spouses, and I am so grateful for the sacrifices they often make and think about how long they must be away from their husbands. I am often filled with gratitude and perspective. I *get* to live this life with my beautiful family and my handsome husband. Even when life isn't perfect (as it so often is not), I know that it could be so much worse. My life could have been so much worse at so many points along this journey. I get to thank God that this broken road has had so many tow trucks and roadside assistance along the way!

Once I was able to get through the pain of the recovery from surgery, I could then go through the mourning and loss of my mom, which was so much tougher to bear emotionally than the surgery had been physically. I miss her so much every single day. She continues to be part of my heart. She is my North Star, and I oftentimes find myself taking a moment to pause from parenting my two girls, looking at various situations before I react to look up and ask, "What would ReRe do?" She always admitted that she knew she was not perfect, but she always made sure to tell me that she was the best mom I was ever going to have! And she was absolutely 100% right!

Saying Goodbye

We had to wait until September of 2020 to hold a small service in Mom's memory because of hefty COVID-19 restrictions. She had wished for a burial at sea instead of a traditionally formal funeral mass, so we held a beautiful ceremony to dedicate a prayer bench in her memory with the Sisters of Mercy on land, and then we headed out on the Never Enuf 2 for the actual burial.

We waited until the following summer when those COVID-19 restrictions were loosened to give my mom, our beautiful ReRe, a proper send-off. We held a Phillies-themed celebration of life in Mom's honor at the local VFW with appearances by former players and a special guest of honor, the Phillie Phanatic himself. We celebrated her love and legacy, told plenty of famous ReRe stories, and cherished the opportunity to properly celebrate her life in a way we all knew would make her smile.

I remember seeing the Phanatic pick up Julia and my niece at the same time, dancing to oldies music, and thinking how much Mom would have loved it. We were sad she wasn't with us physically, but to hear the stories of how she impacted so many lives, we all knew she would continue to live on in so many ways. While my heart was still hurting at the loss of her, my head was relatively calm for the remainder of 2020.

The heartache of losing mom honestly hurt more than the headache of the brain surgeries. I miss her to this day. Some women say, "Oh, my mom is my best friend!" My mom and I didn't have that kind of relationship, and that's the way it was meant to be. We had a mother-daughter relationship that rivaled most. She knew my peers were meant to be my best friends, and the relationship we had was so much more than that. She was my protector, my advocate, my disciplinarian, my role model, and my consoler. She was my mom because I relished her love, needed her support on multiple levels, and required her ability to keep me in line while making sure I still felt cared for.

I looked up to her in so many ways. I still do, but that's largely in part because she's my angel, and I'm always praying to her and asking her to walk beside me and inspire me. My mom was a trailblazer. She was wicked smart, wouldn't take any BS from anyone, could make just about anyone laugh even if they were trying not to, and had a heart the size of a small continent. I regret that my girls didn't get enough time on this earth with her to hear some of her famous ReRe stories about growing up in her large family, about how she found her own deep faith and decided to follow her calling to become an associate with the Sisters of Mercy, and about her experiences as a woman breaking down stereotypes and barriers in so many areas of her life.

She didn't do anything halfway. Except maybe the New York Times Crossword Puzzle—she did that in erasable pen, which I thought was amusing, but even that she would fiercely tackle almost to completion on a weekly basis with dogged determination. When she paid attention to you, she gave you her undivided, wholehearted attention. When she joined a committee at church, she volunteered to be the coordinator (and later in life made an even bigger commitment as an Associate Sister of Mercy!).

When she wanted to embarrass me during my formative years, she made sure I was thoroughly embarrassed (especially in front of my friends). When she threw a party, she threw a *party*. When she wanted to give a lecture, she made sure I left shaking in my boots. Because as cool, calm, and collected as she usually was, when she employed her stern "Mom voice," she wanted me to know that I had crossed the line! However, consequences and punishments were always characterized as "firm but fair," and rightfully so.

Mom's stern and firm side was only out of necessity for her in the role of disciplinarian. Otherwise, boy, did she know how to have fun and make me feel like the center of her universe. When she hugged me, my troubles faded, and she made me feel as though I was the most precious gift God had given her.

Her ability to convey pride and encouragement was second to none. Her capacity as a trained counselor to acutely listen and show empathy was unparalleled. She oftentimes joked she must have a sign written on her face saying, "Tell me your problems" because even complete strangers would confess their issues to her, not knowing that she was a social worker by trade!

She was a true believer in "small world" stories. Nine times out of ten, if you went with her to any local restaurant, sporting event, or other venue, she would start talking to the server, other partygoers, or strangers and find less than six degrees of separation from someone in common that my mother knew or was related to. Not at all surprising given our large Irish Catholic family and the long reach of my mom's influence as a volunteer and worker in the community. They called her the "Mayor of 62nd Street Beach" because everybody knew Marie, and Marie knew everybody.

My brain may have trouble with long-term memory details, yes, but I honestly cannot recall a single time she ever told me, "I don't care." Perhaps it was the combination of genuine, unconditional mother's love alongside the skilled counselor in her that enabled her to remain so compassionate even in the most temper-testing moments. She always gave me the opportunity (as ridiculous as whatever the conversation or conflict may have been) to speak through to completion. She would repeat what she had heard, "If I'm hearing you correctly, you are telling me… Tell me why? Tell me what else?"

I can communicate with my girls now with such emotional awareness and competence because my parents taught my brother and me the immense importance and power of the "I" statement— "I think," "I feel," "I need," "I don't like__ because." They modeled the example and taught us that starting a sentence with "You" will almost always initiate a confrontational, defensive, and counterproductive conversation. The "I" statements they ingrained in me early on have worked with the girls by eliciting less defensiveness and finger-pointing right off the bat with a greater likelihood of conflict resolution.

Managing the emotional ups and downs of this journey has required a lot of talk about feelings, and as expected, the stress of my situation has at times led to conflict between the sisters. I needed a lot of the tools from the toolbox my parents equipped me with. In addition to the "I" statements, they taught me the power of "positive reinforcement" as opposed to negative consequences for behavior—something I still use with the girls today.

Instead of saying, "If you take that toy from your sister again, you are going to your room!" I say, "If you can go the full day without taking stuff from your sister, I will let you have a special movie night." Now that I am old enough to realize it, that sounds an awful lot like bribery—but it has influenced how I keep the girls more positively motivated as opposed to punished negatively. Bribery or not, Mom knew what she was doing, and I smile each time I employ her tactics and they work! Such is how I approach most parenting situations with my girls now, asking myself, *What would ReRe do?*

Mom believed in karma. And somewhere up in His kingdom, I know that she gets a chuckle each time one of my daughters tests my temper with stubbornness or makes my heart stop because of an intense on-the-field-of-play injury. All the same things I put her through. And as Reagan, our older daughter, approaches dating age, my mom is laughing her butt off waiting for the carousel of boys that are about to come asking to take our daughter out. She's probably thinking, *I hope they all ride motorcycles and have mohawks, Ris! Just you wait, she is going to give you a few sleepless nights and you've earned every one of them.*

I look at my girls with such pride and joy as I pass along her legacy of being fearlessly fiery, bold, brave, and independent. She showed me what it means to have boundless and deep faith, to think for and stand up for not only myself, but for any injustices in this world where I could make a difference. She taught me to make a difference wherever I could, that women could break down any and all barriers, that kindness is free, and that you never know what somebody else is going through. She taught me, especially in the last months struggling with her own illness, that to get through my own struggles, I would need to let go and let God. And that He would unfailingly hold me in the palm of His hands.

Even during the times growing up when we disagreed or I felt I was being treated unfairly and I would make my displeasure known, she always said, "Well, Ris, I'm the best Mom you're ever gonna get." Just like that. And she was. She was the best mom I could have ever asked for and made me who I am today.

I'm so grateful for all that she gave me, how she loved me, how much she cherished me from birth right up until her very last days. She could barely even breathe the words, "I love you," but I knew, and my heart was full. She would have gone to the ends of the earth for me, and I know she is the head of multiple committees up in heaven, having worked connections and become a heavenly kind of mayor in some capacity, putting herself in a better position to work her magic on her crew back here.

    I know must've gained influence early on, everybody knowing Marie and all, because my brain surgery went smoothly, recovery was smooth, and things were quiet for the remainder of 2020. The stars then began aligning as if she'd pulled an entire committee of angels together and orchestrated a move just for us, knowing we might be facing some challenges in 2021 that would require some much-needed support.

Brain Frustration and Family Relocation

As I mentioned, the change that came towards the end of 2020 was that I started having partial/breakthrough seizures despite having already undergone what was supposed to have been the "curative" surgery. It was incredibly frustrating, to say the least, and the doctors once again had to tweak my medications because some levels were low for unknown reasons. In January of 2021, I experienced a flurry of more seizure activity, and it was clear that the cure the doctors provided really wasn't much of a cure after all.

Jim and I decided that it was finally time to think about returning closer to family and closing the chapter in our story of our time in Cooperstown. He began the journey of looking for work in Pennsylvania and New Jersey, and along with all her angels, we had our beloved ReRe working to help pull something together for us. It was a new unknown for us, having to figure out moving with our family, and trying to figure out the best places for my medical care. And even though we could have become angry or anxious, we trusted that God was going to provide, and we remained positive.

As we continued to look and while the pandemic was still in full ridiculous swing, and despite the minor breakthrough episodes I was still having, I found myself regularly putting my newfound attitude of gratitude into action. While everyone was talking about frontline workers as deserving all the praise, as I mentioned before, I found myself immeasurably grateful for the grocery store workers and thanked them regularly. They had to show up every single day, and because of their faithfulness to their job, we were all able to get food and feed our families, and that is a hero to me. The same goes for the mailman, the gas station attendant, and so many more.

People are often so quick to complain, and I know that I have been guilty of this as well. But saying the simple words "thank you" as recognition for help is entirely free. We can offer those kind words with little to no effort, so why wouldn't we? Consumer complaint lines, people choosing to rant at the manager, yelling at the nearest young associate at a retail store—it's an easy temptation to be rude and angry. But recognizing someone for doing a great job has a hugely positive impact on that person and their whole day.

Sometimes, when we choose to be positive and effectively share some of that encouragement, as my father has often been incredible about doing by sending letters of recognition to businesses on behalf of a positive experience, there is always the possibility of a reward in response. Now, I am not saying you should have a positive outlook on life and provide encouragement and kindness expecting anything in return, but it is just something that can occasionally come as a nice bonus. It is God's way of rewarding those who treat His children with love, kindness, and mercy.

Research has shown that being kind is good for the body and the mind, also! Being kind boosts levels of serotonin and dopamine, neurotransmitters in the brain that give you those "feel-good" feelings of satisfaction and well-being. Endorphins, which are your body's natural painkiller, are also released. Kindness is also good for the heart, both metaphorically and physically, since showing acts of kindness releases oxytocin, which releases nitric oxide, which dilates your blood vessels, thus reducing your blood pressure and improving your heart health. Thinking about this in the long term, if we get our children at a young age to associate helping others with positive feelings, it will improve the lives of others *and* be beneficial for their long-term health. A genuine win-win situation!

The power of being positive and having a good attitude and a grateful heart can be so very fulfilling for the receiver of even a small kindness, that hopefully they will then pass it along as well. Just think of something as simple as asking the mailman on a hot day if he'd like a bottle of water. You might be surprised at how many delivery people are shocked when you demonstrate an interest in helping them and providing acts of kindness during their busy days.

No matter the situation, no matter the day, and no matter the reason, it is such an important part of life to be encouraging and kind. The kindness of a stranger is something so unexpected, yet much needed in this world. A stranger who demonstrates kindness is not likely to look for anything in return; they simply want to be kind and lighten the day of another. When you show kindness and appreciation to a stranger, you are telling them that they are important enough to deserve such an acknowledgment.

Through this selfless act, you demonstrate that they are seen, heard, and valued, and you may give them the ability to pick themselves up and carry any weight through the rest of their day. Because, again, you just never know what anyone is going through. I have a note written on my girls' bathroom mirror that reads, "Be kind whenever possible, and it is ALWAYS possible." So, just be kind.

I think it was by no small miracle that we moved into our dream home in Bucks County in August of 2021, and it was within ten minutes of Jim's sister and her family, and then less than an hour from most of my own extended family. As fate would have it, within just a few months of us moving, my brother moved into the same town as us *and* Jim's parents relocated to the area within a fifteen-minute drive, as well. When we moved, we had hoped to enlist the help of more family support if needed, but now we would really have a full army on our side!

After the move, we were finally able to honor my mom in the most appropriate way possible (we had to wait for COVID-19 restrictions to loosen). We had a Phillies-style block party in Sea Isle in her honor. It was filled with so much love, laughter, and of course, the Phillie Phanatic and crab fries! We were able to come together and cry as we told our favorite ReRe stories while obviously sporting our Phillies gear while watching slideshows of our fondest memories of her and even dancing to some of her favorite oldies tunes.

I was able to find a new neurologist after the move, and things were relatively quiet for the rest of 2021. We got the girls involved in some great extracurricular activities that they both enjoyed. Reagan thrives in her horseback riding, and it seems you couldn't throw a stick in Bucks County without hitting a horse farm, so that was a fortunate situation. And little Julia, well, she is the smallest but also fiercest in her karate class and smiles the most as she runs up and down the soccer field, even when she is getting knocked down (and gets right back up, like her proud mama).

Jim was able to get established with his new group as a reliable and hard-working partner, but those long hours were so much more bearable with all the family backup we had nearby. It was easy to have Jim's parents helping us to get out of the house to go over for visits at my brother's house or to take the girls to his sister's house. We were able to be present for so many more milestones instead of just having to say, "Sorry, the drive is just too far, and we're snowed in again." Trips to Sea Isle didn't require eight separate bathroom stops and a cooler full of snacks anymore, and we could even make weekend trips whenever we wanted, even on a whim!

Angels, Angst, and an Army of Assistance

Things stayed quiet even into 2022, other than a few occasional medication dosage tweaks when levels looked a little low. The usual happy stress of the holidays behind us, we got back into the school routine and things were off to quite a happy and hopeful new year, indeed. But then, just like the shock of a bucket of cold water poured over my head, and yet another reminder in life not to take anything for granted, I had another blackout seizure. This time, I was driving Reagan to a friend's house close by.

So, on January 10, with no warning, none of my usual pre-seizure auras or funny feelings, BANG, it just hit me. Thank God yet again (and of course, my angel, ReRe, who is always with me and watching over me, sending beautiful rainbows after every storm), both Reagan and I were totally okay physically. I hit a curb and a stop sign, but what is more amazing is that I did not hit anyone else. Of all the things that could have happened, all the pain that could have been inflicted upon us in that accident, God had protected us, and our bodies were fine.

Despite how scary it must have been for her, because she is so incredible, Reagan knew that I was having a seizure and was able to get out her phone to call her friend. Maybe it wasn't 911 or her dad, but she still called someone who could help. She is only twelve years old, after all. Thank God, again, for the fact that she had the presence of mind and the capability to make that call for help! Her friend's mom then called 911 for us and came to the scene to wait until paramedics arrived.

I have no memory of any of this event, or the following day and a half in the hospital (eighteen full hours that I have zero recollection of). It doesn't seem that this seizure was triggered by anything other than my Scarecrow brain. This one just happened. Maybe it was going to happen regardless of where I was, and so I am thankful that God put Reagan in the car with me at that time because, otherwise, I would have been alone with no one who could help me. What's even worse, I could have been driving Julia from school, and she certainly doesn't know how to stay calm in those types of situations or who she's supposed to call in an emergency. God really is a divine orchestrator, masterfully conducting every movement in the musical of our lives.

After this seemingly random episode, it became quite difficult to calm the girls' fears about what to think of these episodes. After all, we had all thought this was taken care of after the surgery. Reagan had gotten lulled into a sense of security, much like I had, as if the episodes had officially become a thing of the past, a genuine lifetime ago. But then, BAM! Talk about a very unfriendly reality check, and for Reagan, this was particularly harrowing considering it happened while we were on the road.

Even once my license was officially reinstated, she still was a little afraid to get in the car with me alone for a very long time, which is entirely understandable. Even now, anything more than about ten to fifteen miles away in distance makes her a little uneasy. She even makes me text her when I am heading out by myself someplace and when I have arrived at my destination safely. She really is such a wonderful kid, and while there are moments when it is unfortunate that aspects of her life require such adult mentalities, it is still such an incredible blessing to see how mature she is in these areas.

From her perspective, though, things are just as uncertain and out of control as they are for me, but she isn't a mind reader, and so she doesn't know how I am feeling physically, the auras, the tiredness, or whether I am feeling at all "off" at the time, and so she has a greater feeling of powerlessness. Especially since that January episode came literally out of nowhere and with absolutely no warning at all.

For Julia, being of an age to better grasp the gravity of everything, she has so many questions, which are wonderful, and which we answer as best we can when we have answers. Sometimes, though, all I can offer is, "Only God knows what will happen", or something as simple as, "These things just sometimes happen, peanut." For a six-and-a-half-year-old, sometimes that is just not enough of an answer.

Even though we are a family deeply rooted in faith and have always imparted that same mentality to our girls, when faced with a situation where Mommy's health appears to be in jeopardy, it is too much to simply ask a small child to just have faith. In an ideal world, that would be enough, but we live in a fallen world, and kids need more reassurance. She fears the dark sometimes still, so the idea of telling her to just not be afraid of Mommy needing to be carted off in the ambulance again just doesn't make sense at all. She needs more love and support in these fears, and we regularly do our best to explain things and provide as much information as is appropriate to help her feel more at ease.

Things are a little bit different with Reagan, as she is older and already has a better understanding of the entire situation. She has seen me through so many scary moments, so many times taken away in an ambulance, time spent in the hospital. She was only ten years old when I had my full craniotomy, so she has a comprehensive understanding of what I have been through and the journey our family has walked together. My almost teenage girl is my angel for having saved me after that accident, and all I can do now is continue to ask her to pray with me, to trust me, to trust the doctors, and to trust all of the angels watching over us, and most definitely my own personal, on-call angel, ReRe, on my shoulder, keeping an eye on us all.

At the time, we were still with Capital Health, which is a smaller regional hospital. However, the neurologists that Jim and I met with were very confident that I was a good candidate for the Neuropace device, which was an implant that could monitor, detect, and respond to my seizures automatically and in real time without me even noticing. It was sort of like a pacemaker, but for the brain, which not only sounded promising for better long-term control going forward but also like I could tell people I was a bionic woman of sorts! I would still need to take my medications, but those could be decreased over time. The most recent seizure itself had been mind-blowing, both literally and figuratively.

Learning that I could possibly be a good candidate for this kind of device made me so incredibly hopeful but at the same time, it sounded like the initial implementation was going to be an exceptionally tedious process. I would have to undergo an extensive amount of testing first (oh great, not the Guinea pig process again!), then I'd have to get more MRIs, more PET scans, functional MRIs, Neuropsych evaluations, and that whole shebang all over again! Undoubtedly, I was dreading the thought of all the testing and hoops that required jumping through, but the thought of possibly moving forward free from the fear of seizures (or at least not knowing if I was having one because, with the aid of the device, obliviousness would be bliss) was very promising.

Still, I couldn't quite get past all the testing, the physical and emotional toll it would take, not to mention just how long it would take just to get everything scheduled. It would take months upon months. It brought back all the memories of what I had already gone through back in 2019 and 2020. Didn't we get this all figured out already? The doctor said I would need to do, just like back in 2019, another series of inpatient seizure monitoring.

This doctor, however, didn't want to do intracranial monitoring like in 2019. Instead, they would use depth electrodes, which would be slightly less invasive, though the seizures themselves would still cause all the usual brain fuzziness and overall lost pathways. I thought perhaps that was a reasonable, small price to pay to hopefully get that cure I'd wanted for so long.

This was all going to be necessary to match the device to my specific brainwaves so that the doctor could continually program it as she got readouts of my brain activity. When they did the monitoring before my temporal lobe resection in 2020, they had noticed "noise" on the left side of my brain but were unable to determine if that seizure activity came from independent charges or just aftershocks from the lesion that they zeroed in on and then removed.

There was a possibility that the seizure behind the wheel was caused by the left side demonstrating that it was independent, also. Only, it really wasn't. Turns out that just a few days later, I tested positive for COVID-19. My seizure threshold had been in the tank, and I was susceptible at the time.

And, yet once again, my license was suspended. Only this time, we were surrounded by an army of family that we had been blessed with in our move. My in-laws were of immense support and could be on-call at the last moment's notice for anything and everything we might have needed—for pickups, drop-offs, or even just help with getting to doctor's appointments. My dad, whenever he visited, always offered to take me anywhere I needed.

He called himself my personal Uber driver. In fact, he gave me one great little tip he'd learned a while back. See, in addition to being quite the MacGyver who can fix just about anything and a master with duct tape, never backing down from a puzzling repair, he is also a savvy and experienced world traveler.

He has given me such an amazing amount of support over the years and, of course, the usual fatherly wisdom that a daughter might often expect. "Measure twice, cut once," which I couldn't help but think in 2020 when the surgeons were about to dig into my brain. In this case with my license, when I first needed to use Uber, he suggested that if I got a driver who was nice and reliable, I could ask them if they might ever be available for hire outside of the Uber app. That way, I could find my very own personal Uber driver (outside of my dad, of course)! I did end up finding a very kind gentleman who, upon hearing my story, gave me his card and said he would absolutely help if needed! I would just need to give him slightly more than a moment's notice!

Julia and my nephew attended the same preschool, so my brother and sister-in-law took turns bringing her to and from school when Jim was not able to. And, in those times when they couldn't take a shift, the teachers and even the principal, Miss Amber, from Julia's school would be so kind as to bring her home. We knew, and they knew, that they didn't have to do that, but I had shown my appreciation for them so much in the past that they were happy to return the favor.

I can't help but look back on this time that could have been the most discouraging time in my life and simply smile at the encouragement and support I received. People literally came out of everywhere to help and support me, and it just goes to show that there is so much kindness in the world, and it just encourages me to do the same as often as I possibly can.

All the terrific teachers had become very familiar with my consistent motto of "Gratitude is everything!" On a semi-weekly basis, I had been sending lunches or Starbucks to the school as a pick-me-up for the staff because they deserve so much more appreciation than just on Teacher Appreciation Day. Teaching today, what with technology and curriculum demands ever-changing, can be such a challenge, and it often requires so much dedication and time spent outside of the classroom to ensure success for students. Teachers sometimes spend more time with the kids than some parents do each week. They play such a vital role in helping build and shape the minds of our children for generations to come to create a better tomorrow! How could I not be eternally grateful for all they do?

So, from January through March, we just kept swimming (like Dory, remember?). They added one more medication, making for a total of four, and I kept on waking up, feet on the floor, filled with gratitude, and so entirely thankful for all the help of everyone around us. That episode, though, was significant enough, and we were so close to the experts at the University of Pennsylvania that we decided we could afford to seek a second opinion on the Neuropace device.

Getting the second opinion was to learn how to get access to the best technology for diagnosing and treating epilepsy, including the option of a laser ablation which had been previously discussed as a possibility. That had been brought up as a possible solution when we had been at Rochester Medicine. This decision to switch was both a "no-brainer," but also a "for the sake of my brain-er." I did fear that getting an appointment at Penn with a new neurologist would take a long time, though. We were able to utilize some of the connections that my aunt in healthcare had, and I was able to get an initial virtual visit that April.

The new doctor was incredibly thorough, and we knew right away that despite the long and somewhat stressful wait for the initial appointment, she'd been worth it all the while, and that we'd made the right decision to go with her. She spent over an hour with us, explaining everything, and making sure we understood. We planned for her to get the intracranial EEG records from Rochester to determine if my seizures were only of right brain origin, and whether or not she felt I would indeed be a potential candidate for the laser ablation surgery. But a multidisciplinary panel would meticulously review my case and carefully decide what course of action to take next, and I would still need to do the surgery for intracranial seizure monitoring once again to confirm.

Preparation, Perseverance, and the Panel's Decision

Anything involving records and the transferring of medical information between institutions can feel a bit like *Days of Our Lives*—"like sands through the hourglass." Add a slow-moving system with the need to coordinate the busy schedules of the specialists who comprised the multidisciplinary panel in charge of overseeing and reviewing my case, and I now was facing a three-month wait before the doctor told me I could expect to hear anything. I was back to summoning my best waiting game face.

Three months might not seem like a long time, but when it is a waiting game for my unsettled brain, and all I want is answers and solutions, three months is an eternity, it seems. If the records and testing showed that less invasive surgery wouldn't work, the panel would consider a RE-resection (which would be a full craniotomy again). Jim told the doctor that recovery after the 2020 surgery wasn't "too bad," but he wasn't the one with the massive headache after having his head cut open! And, though I do love him dearly, he may or may not be known to crumble into a pitiful mess at the first sign of a man-cold.

It was at this point that Reagan began to express that she was having some anxiety and worry about the thought of me having to have two more procedures. Considering the trauma of having been in the car and needing to be the one to call for rescue in the January accident, she was doing remarkably well, and this kind of apprehension and anxiety was completely understandable. She had so many questions about when it would happen, what it would look like, and how recovery might compare to the previous surgery. These were normal questions to ask, and so we did our best to walk through the answers we knew and explain the need to have faith in the things that we didn't have answers for. Through these conversations, we all sort of started to question whether this procedure would work at this time, also.

Around Easter, I once again took the time to really reflect on everything, and then especially during the holiest of seasons, I dedicated a great deal of time looking upward, with a new perspective thinking about how Christ so willingly suffered. Yeah, my aches and pains were pretty bad at times, but they were nothing compared to what He went through. I trusted that He had sent me on this journey, holding me in the palm of His hands and sending angels when I needed them most. He created me with all the strength, hope, and love that I needed to overcome these challenges. I felt so grateful to be surrounded by love and so many more family members since we had moved. I was genuinely blessed beyond words.

I'd done this surgery thing before, and I could do it again. Heck, maybe I could even get a commemorative plaque in the surgery center or get to sign a wall of fame for the three- or four-timers club! I would just need to take those three months and whatever followed one minute, hour, day at a time, just like I'd done (and continue to do) with my sobriety. I was able to experience the peace of accepting the things I cannot change and the courage to change what I can, and I kept looking up for the rainbows because I knew that ReRe was right beside me every step of the way. Each of my previous challenges was a building block in preparation for the next challenge laid out before me on my journey. Though it was still not my favorite thing in the world, I had gotten very accustomed to waiting and practicing better patience with the process of being an epilepsy patient going through this type of pre-surgical process.

The doctor requested some significantly higher resolution MRI imaging (3T and 7T, "T" being Tesla), which I ended up getting done at the end of July. Perhaps the stress of it all had me a little on edge, but in those months between March and September, I needed to use my emergency medication for mild auras that thankfully never generalized and that didn't persist beyond a bit of a funny taste and some dizziness.

The panel was scheduled to meet in mid-August and my appointment at Penn was set for after Labor Day. These mild "blips" could have been an opportunity to freak out, panic, or even become pessimistic. Ironically, they were most likely just the result of anxiously awaiting my fate as placed in the panels' hands. So, I took these "blips" for what they were—blips on the radar. And since I couldn't control what they were going to decide, I chose to focus on each moment for what it was, preciously placed right in front of me. I made sure I was taking good care of myself first and foremost, and then I was back to the serenity prayer, of course, because the panel's decision was out of my control, and I was ready to accept whatever may come.

I had been bracing myself for the news that the imaging showed I would need more surgery, but I was prepared mentally and I had peace in my heart and mind because even if these blips were more than that, God had sent me on this journey purposefully allowing me to pick up so many tools already. I would be able to handle whatever He had planned for me next. Whatever piece of music, I had trained to play it. There was no mountain I couldn't climb, seeing as I already had the endurance because of my training.

And, as we soaked up the sun during those waning days of summer, I enjoyed the company of the SIC 62nd beach crew and did my best to demonstrate patience and peace with the girls. This time wouldn't have been possible without their favorite fun aunts and uncles who always spoil them with extra ice cream (ahem, Aunt T and Uncle B!).

We did our usual back-to-school shopping excitedly, and I told them, with full transparency, that I believed good things were in store for us. I reassured them that we should all trust the panel, our angels, especially ReRe, and God that things would work out. We saw our fair share of rainbows over the summer and felt the positivity as we waited, and I remained seizure-free throughout the entire summer!

So, Jim and I made the drive down to Penn, and the doctor told us that the panel had reviewed everything and my entire case history in great detail. It was probably the most positive report I could have gotten. She conveyed that the consensus was that unless I had another blackout episode like in January, no further surgery was warranted. They said that the risks of trying to "clean up" any of the resectioned area with another craniotomy far outweighed the benefits when I was showing a great deal of stability on the most recently added medication. And, by that point, I was going on roughly eight months being seizure-free, and I had just gotten my driving privileges reinstated! Jim and I were able to celebrate such a wonderful victory together!

I must say, even after seventeen years of being married to that man, I am still madly in love with him, and I would love him no matter his profession. He would make an all-star professional chef, too, and we are treated to his cooking on most weekends, even after some of his most labor-intensive work weeks in the operating rooms. What a gift to be able to sit around the table as a family, savoring his delicious meals.

I can see how God put us on such a perfect path toward each other for a reason, especially given all my medical challenges through the years. As fate would have it, I fell in love with a man who practices medicine! Not just that, either, but also that he is a man I've known since I was just barely a teenager, and he's my best friend. I'm blessed to be able to say that I met both of my best friends in middle school.

Cue the *Jeopardy* music...the waiting game had ended, and we met with the doctor for the results. In the opinion of the panel, it was determined that I could by all accounts be viewed as having achieved quite a favorable outcome from the initial resection. And, outside the episode in January, I am doing quite well. The medication adjustment the doctor made, she indicated, should help with preventing any further of those mild auras, and if that continues to work, we could maybe even start working towards tapering off some of the other meds, getting me down to a fewer number of meds overall.

Let the Music Play On

When I left the appointment that day, I was filled with relief, positivity, faith, and overwhelming gratitude in my heart. I am so grateful for all the love and prayers that have been sent from all over the world, for the grace of God, that He has given me the strength and peace to keep living this life with my amazing family and so many more tomorrows full of hope. When I mentioned in previous pages how important it is to understand that we are not the ones to author our own lives or write the music, I said so from a place of experience.

At times I thought it was my job to be in control of everything—to not just wake up and play His music, but to write it, conduct it, and dwell on how poorly I had played in concerts past instead of just enjoying the piece of music He has written for me to play. To wake up every day with joy in my heart, grateful that I get to play, blessed to be a part of the orchestra is so much more fulfilling and what He has wished for me since my baptism. Sometimes the music is sad and sometimes it is at a frenzied pace—but other times the music is so utterly joyful that it is beyond comprehension.

I have free will and can make my own choices every day, especially when it comes to how I treat those around me. God has shown me over and over that it is not my job to hold that pen or to try to be anything other than who He made me to be. It's not my responsibility to be in charge or in control of anything other than my own attitude about the path set before me each day. Had I tried to take ultimate control and defy His plan by denying surgery, or defying treatment, I could have been gone a long time ago. Instead, I learned that it is okay to put down the pen, trust in the plan set before me, and honestly enjoy the beauty of God's blessings big and small with gratitude. And I am still here, and I am honored to have gotten the opportunity to share this story with you.

While my brain may always be a little bit damaged, my spirit will never be broken, for I am beyond blessed. I feel that God has fully prepared me for whatever hills and valleys and songs are on the path next that He has planned for me. Even if I am not musically inclined and may not follow the same rhythm as everyone else, it is just an honor to be a player in the orchestra of God's glorious story.

Being able to play the music He has written with faith, kindness, and a sense of purpose is what helps to heal me every single day. This world can be such a discouragingly negative place, and it seems horrifically broken at times, with messages of war, disease, and death flooding our eyes and ears, and politics causing endless divides on every side. At times it is easy to feel damaged and discouraged by all this ugliness around us, emotionally, physically, and spiritually. But as my mom always said, "Everybody's going through something." By that logic, it means not one of us is alone in our struggles.

James tells us that we should consider it joy when we face trials of any kind because that is what creates in us a stronger faith, which produces perseverance and that is how God guides us through difficult times, with His strength and perseverance (James 1:2-3). Alas, the trials, brokenness, and damage we each may experience will occasionally leave us feeling vulnerable and like we might be playing the music of life slightly off-key, but that is okay. And while I have no ultimate "curative" temporal lobe resective surgery solutions to offer, I hope that through these pages, you have been able to find a little joyful, hopeful melody or message.

Perhaps that little melody change is the boost you needed to allow you to find peace or the encouragement you needed to push through a difficult season in your own life. Whether you are struggling with addiction or feel helpless watching someone you know and love struggle. Perhaps you are living with the wild uncertainty caused by epilepsy or are struggling with another medical condition causing distress.

Whatever the case may be, I hope you have been able to see that it is possible to find positivity and little pockets of peace in this crazy thing called life. And that even when things don't go as planned, it is still possible to find happiness with whatever God has blessed you with, whether it feels like a blessing or not. And with your blessings, let it be possible to spread even the smallest blessings to others as well. Just because we may feel helpless at times, that doesn't mean we can't be helpful to others.

Above all else, I hope that the message gained from my story is that you see each of us can look inward and upward EVERY. SINGLE. DAY. I hope you see it is possible to choose love and kindness, strength over struggle, faith over fear, counting each of our blessings before our burdens as we play our music just as it was beautifully written for each of our journeys. As we each heal our brokenness and damage, we will be playing one incredible soundtrack to this amazing gift God has given us called life! And, above all else, when in doubt, may we all be on the lookout for beautiful rainbows!

Epilogue

As I mentioned, I do love to exercise every day on our rowing machine. I have been consistent with these bright and early workouts since we got the machine before the resective brain surgery in early 2020. We're talking about daily 4-5 miles of rowing for 4 years. I also mentioned being a softball player in high school. I was the catcher and that spine-straining crouched position was no joke for four years on varsity. I still love to play ball on the beach with the girls. Reagan especially has a great arm.

Well, between playing ball, my age, and most recently the four years of daily rowing, all that spine-straining motion took its toll and God decided to throw yet another curve ball my way just as I had completed this manuscript for final edits and proofreading. Turns out my surgery survival story wasn't over after all.

This latest curve ball, oddly (and so very gratefully enough) had nothing to do with my brain. Perhaps as a reminder that I need to slow down, or just to keep me on my toes. Previously when I was exercising and busy with my usual mama bear household tasks, I experienced intermittent lower back soreness which became more nagging over the summer. I was not to be deterred by a little pain and continued to row my five miles every day and listen to my throwback jamz since it was my routine, essential for my mental health, peace and prayer. Plus, I still hadn't found a running partner. Or gone insane.

Since by now you know that I have experienced some pretty grueling pain, you can imagine my threshold/tolerance level is pretty high and I didn't think anything was wrong other than a pulled muscle. So, like any brain surgery survivor, I would occasionally just throw an icy/hot patch on and keep rowing and doing my mama bear stuff.

In late January my body finally screamed *"Hey dummy!! Somethings wrong here!!..."* and what I thought was at first just a pulled hamstring, turned into shooting pains down my left leg and a few days after onset I began experiencing numbness in my left foot and could barely get myself dressed in the morning.

Once again, thank God Jim is in the Ortho profession! Seeing that I was displaying true discomfort and pain made him do a double take. He knew that if I was complaining it must be serious. Jim made a phone call, pulled a favor and I quickly got in to see the spine specialist, Dr. Cairone, at the office the following morning. That expediency right there made all the long on-call weekends Jim sometimes has to work worthwhile. And I realized how fortunate I was to get the family treatment that would otherwise land most people in the ER on such short notice.

After a few stretches and reflex tests, Dr. C told me he suspected a bulged disc was causing the trouble. He prescribed a short course steroid to see if it would "calm things down" but also laid out various possible options for treatment dependent on the MRI results. If the short course of steroids didn't provide any relief, he thought a steroid injection might help. And if that couldn't help, perhaps an epidural. At the initial visit, we briefly discussed perhaps down the road exploring surgery if these interventional steps didn't help. I knew I was in good hands and trusted Dr. Cairone's plan going forward. It was a relief just to know that I wasn't going crazy! Plus, he's just a genuinely nice guy who didn't rush through the exam.

Amazingly, I got right in for my lumbar MRI that Friday morning. Again, the perks and blessings of expedited scheduling with connections! Jim was able to log in and see the MRI pictures before Dr. Cairone even had a chance to give me a call. Spine troubles not being Jim's area of expertise, he couldn't make a full diagnosis other than *"something doesn't look right"*. Ha. I could have told Jim that! It's not like my pain was just manifesting out of nowhere. His esteemed colleague Dr. C, however, gave him the heads up that surgery would be the best option, seeing as the nerves around my L5/S1 disc were almost completely crushed (hence the shooting pains). The doctor felt like all of the other interventional treatments wouldn't give me any measurable relief and we'd just be prolonging the inevitable.

When I got the phone call from Dr. Cairone to report the results, he then posed the question "So, do you want to get this taken care of?" I didn't hesitate for more than a quick 2.42 seconds (ok 2.5), at the chance for the lumbar decompression/discectomy surgery for my L5S1 disc the following Monday morning! Jim told me he was shocked that I wasn't at all more reluctant. He said *"Wow you must really be in pain! Don't you wanna figure out the logistics, kids, schedule, and whatnot??? Most people take more than 5 seconds to agree to surgery on short notice as if it's no big deal!"* To which I reminded him we could easily figure the schedule out, and we had a lot of support nearby. As for the surgery itself.... definitely a what's-left-of my-brainer-er since first of all, I was experiencing the constant shooting pains and needed some sort of relief. And second of all, *surgery schmurgery*.... what's a little incision in my back compared to a craniotomy!?!!

I couldn't help but find the irony in the situation. That I would definitely need to add epilogue material, about how I wrote a book about surviving brain surgeries only to have it lead to more surgery! And what a pain in the rear it ended up being trying to get it finally finished! Pun totally intended.

The surgery was a success because of the incredible precision and healing hands of Dr. Cairone. Guess he wouldn't want to screw it up with his co-worker's wife on the table, but still the immediate relief I felt was miraculous. To be pain free right away was mind blowing, I couldn't believe it was real! And I even gave some of my friends a chuckle as I provided updates throughout about my post-op recovery to those who were concerned that I might really have a hard time getting back on my feet. Ha.

Risa's guide to back surgery recovery….

Monday: surgery @12:30. Done by 3. I can feel my legs again, wohoo!! Pain, what pain?? Oh, that little incision? Kinda a pain in the rear (haha). Outta the surgery center and home at 3:30 in time for hugs from Julia after getting off the school the bus @4.

Tuesday: Do a full load of laundry, walk the kids to school bus and make a full dinner as usual.

Wednesday: Maybe I overdid it a little yesterday…but nothing some Tylenol can't fix and then I can do the grocery shopping, but I won't lift anything heavier than a gallon of milk at a time, per Dr. C.'s orders!

Thursday: Running more errands albeit not running exactly, because truly… nobody is chasing me

Friday: Shower time, finally! What, did I have surgery or something?

Saturday: Hey Jim, can you ask Dr. C when I'm allowed to get back on the rowing machine? (Joking/totally not joking?) Dr's Response was basically "uh…she crazy?!?! no!"

And that's how post-surgical "pain", recovery and "taking it easy" worked compared to my previous craniotomy! A blessing and a curse I suppose, all that exercise that got me in the pickle in the first place gave me plenty of core strength to make recovery a breeze.

At my follow up, Dr. C recommended waiting until the six-week mark for a return to exercise as usual. And me being largely of the rule-following sort, I wouldn't want to cause any harm to the newly repaired area. It was a good thing I had the surgery when I did, as it appeared from the MRI the discs weren't going to get any better by themselves. In fact at the rate I'd been going and my pain tolerance, stubbornness and willingness to ignore the minor backaches, the situation would have only gotten worse had my leg not started to go numb. Who knows what kind of permanent damage I could have suffered by trying to push through or if the stars hadn't aligned for me to be seen in such a timely manner.

More importantly, I was fortunate that Dr. Cairone was at the helm! I appreciated how quickly he accommodated his schedule for my situation and how expertly he patched me up. He didn't just take away the pain, didn't just do a quick repair on my disc to relieve the shooting pains. He gave me a gift and for that I will always be grateful. Because of his work, soon I could resume the exercise routine I have found so essential to staying balanced, prayerful, and at peace with myself and my disease.

As with all of my previous surgeries and struggles, I received prayers and healing vibes from far and wide. Best of all, my brain cooperated quietly throughout the back surgery curveball, thank God. But perhaps now it's time take my foot off the gas a touch. And *self-knowledge* being of utmost importance to me, I suppose I should listen to the signs. I may have received prayers, but I also received messages of caution in a caring manner. One of my favorite people on the planet whose advice I particularly treasure suggested that although I may want to absorb life all at once, I shouldn't kill myself in the process. I am deeply appreciative of that brand of loving sage advice, and it definitely takes a certain persuasion to get me to ease up. But what am I going to do at 4:30am now, sleep in?!? I kinda enjoy waking up a little blurry-eyed at the crack of dawn!

  I suppose I don't necessarily need to go all out all the time with the strenuous stuff, that it's ok to try new things. Maybe I should even consider *some kind* of lower intensity workouts while remaining grounded, grateful and healthy. Maybe something to jumpstart my heart just enough, I won't know what it feels like to switch things up until I give it a go!

  It's definitely discouraging to have to dial it down for a stubborn and active person like myself who thrives on a certain schedule. Change makes me feel all mixed up! But in the end, I know this tap on the shoulder was just another part of my story. Throughout my life, I've learned that these curveballs happen with purpose. And when they do, I just have to adjust my swing and take the hint that the experience is meant to prepare me for another piece of music yet to be revealed. I feel ready for whatever comes next, I am grateful beyond measure, feel stronger than ever and I'm glad I took a swing at writing all of this, curveballs and all.

  It's not like I am calling the pitches, I'm not the catcher anymore. I just have to wait and see what happens every morning when I step into the batter's box and trust above all else. Taking things down a notch doesn't necessarily have to be a bad thing, either. I will find a new routine that doesn't push the limits but still keeps me sane. Plus, I hear we have some really nice walking (not running!) paths around here for good exercise.

Surgery #1 – August 2019

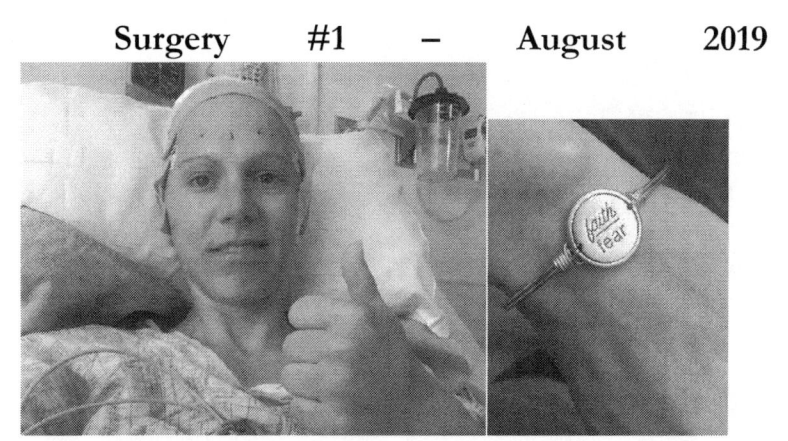

Marking entry points for wires to be threaded and placed directly onto all four lobes

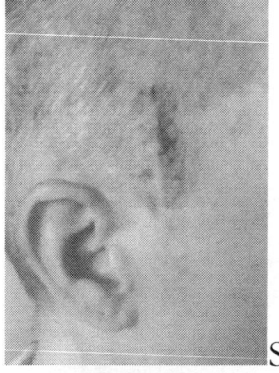

Side view after surgery#1

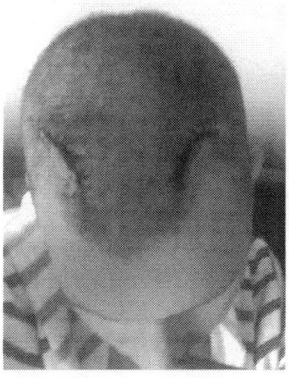

My "horn removal" scars from wires being threaded into my head and onto the brain for seizure monitoring

Surgery #2– January 2020

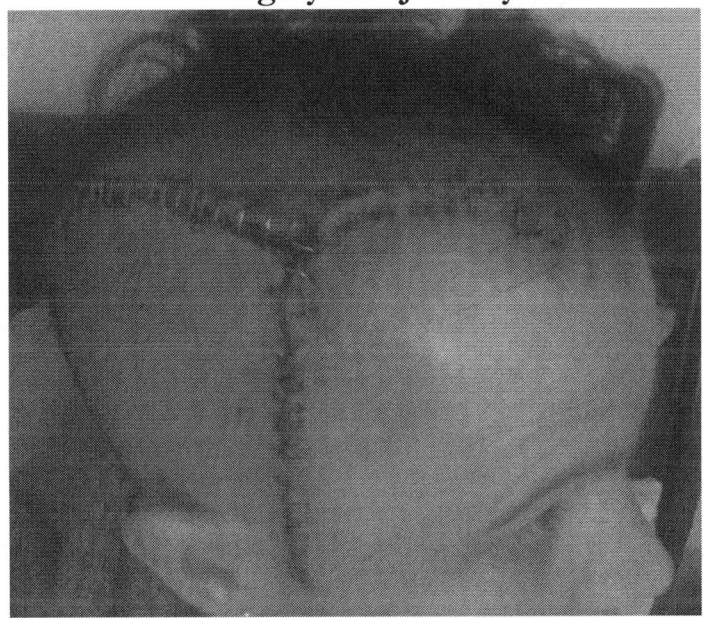

Full craniotomy for right temporal lobe resection

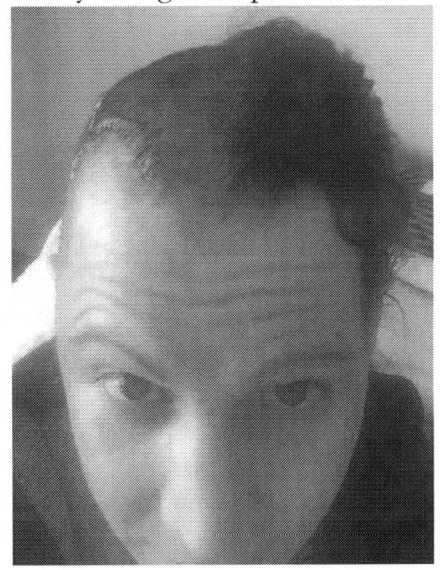

Haircut for surgery, only ½ the head. putting a "bad hair day" into new perspective

A Beautifully Blessed Family

Jim and Risa circa 10th grade

Just Married! 2006

Pre-surgery Nov 2018

Dec 2020

July 2020

July 2021

September 2021 					Christmas 2022

Spring 2023

Dec. 2023    Jan. 2024

JoePa and My Guardian Angel, ReRe

My incredible parents (JoePa & ReRe)

Beautiful Mama/ReRe

Acknowledgments

Thank You God, ReRe and my many angels for keeping me on earth long enough to document this story through to completion, epilogue and all! Through all of my ups and downs, the seizures and surgeries, my rock bottoms and reunions, God and my angels never gave up on me. I suppose because they felt I still had work to do here instead of joining them upstairs. Through all of the waiting, searching, healing and hurting they were always by my side, and it was all worth it for me to be able to get to this very point.

Writing this book has been a dream of mine for a long time. I always knew in my heart that there was a deeper meaning for my trials and survival and that my story could hopefully be of benefit to others. At the very least, I felt compelled to write it for my incredible daughters to use as a resource and hold onto as a testament to the heritage of strength and resilience that exists within them. My girls are my proudest accomplishment and I couldn't have brought them or this book into this world without the help of my hard working and handsome husband.

On that note, to the man who still puts stars in my eyes and tomorrows in my heart. Thank you to my hard-working brilliant and devoted husband, Jim. A broken, repaved wild ride of a road, indeed, my love. If you had told me in seventh grade that we could be living the life we have today I would have told you that you were crazy. If you told me what kind of twists and turns our road would take, that we would come out stronger than I could imagine, I would believe you because we are that good of a team and you have always been of such strong character. Just saying "Thank You" isn't enough. I feel like I owe you my life and more. Thank you for the being the tower of strength I needed to lean on after every seizure, during the hospital stays and especially those long nights in surgery and recovery. I know it wasn't easy for you to put on the brave face watching me struggle, but you got me through and you always have. When I couldn't process the medical info, you could and you never freaked out at how scary any of it sounded. I couldn't ask for a better co-pilot on this road we're traveling. I am in constant awe of your ability to heal others in your professional life full-time while also working overtime at home as our weekend chef, Nintendo master, and chauffeur—all without complaint or needing an IV of coffee. Okay, maybe you do need a lot of coffee. And snacks. Thank you for your encouragement throughout the writing process and allowing me the space and time to pursue this dream even after you had worked full weeks yourself, and for helping me fill in some of the blanks. I can't wait to see where this road takes us next. I'm wearing my seatbelt, for sure. Especially since you're driving a turbo now. I love you and always will.

    To the only other guy who has my heart in this world, my best Dad, JoePa. Thank you for your unconditional love, always. It is because you sent me the writing workshop info that I finally got the right opportunity and "kick in the pants" I needed to step into the batter's box and take a swing at this. More importantly, for my entire life, you have supported every dream, every activity, and stood by me never doubting my abilities or potential because, as you have said countless times, you are "always in my corner." I love you beyond words and can never repay you for all the opportunities you have given me and how you and Mom raised me. You both instilled in me a value system, teaching me about integrity, faith, commitment, service, bravery and love and family first. I am who I am because of you. Thank you for continually giving me your fatherly wisdom, I don't know what I'd do or where I'd be without you. Thank you for believing in me even when I didn't believe in myself. Thank you for forgiving me even when I couldn't forgive myself. I'm sorry for the many heart attacks (minor and major) that I gave you along the way, but payback is a b****, and I'm getting my comeuppance with these two fierce and feisty girls. You are an inspiration of what it means to be committed to faith and family, of service to the community, and true to oneself. Thanks for the long tosses in the backyard way back when and on the beach – because you are the real catch, Dad! And you've caught yourself a mighty fine one yourself. Candita, I'm grateful for your recent presence in our lives. We are so enriched with your light, love and positivity. You and Dad make a fantastic dancing duo and it warms my heart to see his, and your, happy feet on the floor and that smile on his face. Thank you for what you bring to the family!

To my intelligent, fearless, and beautiful daughters, Reagan and Julia. Thank you for giving me purpose in this world and making me the proudest mama on the planet. Thank you for being the fuel in my tank to keep me going on this journey. I had no idea how strong I could be until I had no choice and it's all because of my marvelous motivational kiddos. I was faced with more than a few daunting days but you young ladies are my whole world and I was going to do whatever it meant to keep living for you! You bring me joy each and every day. You are my biggest cheerleaders, having shown so much courage during my seizures, surgeries and hospital stays and encouraging me even when you were scared yourselves. I couldn't have done this without your hugs, the sound of your laughter, your mom coupon books, and your willingness to put up with me at my typing desk for so long. It warms my heart to see so much of ReRe living on in the both of you. I see in you her faith, her determination and confidence, her spirit of giving, and her joy for life, not to mention her spunk! Continue pursuing your passions, following your dreams and aiming high. You are destined for greatness. It is because of you that I get out of bed every day with hope and positivity for the future. I love you to the moon and back, always.

I'm the woman I am today, raising these fierce young ladies because I come from a long line of strong, independent, trailblazing, fearless, faith-filled women. My mother first and foremost, but I'd be remiss if I didn't also recognize and thank the additional women in my life who have held me up in my times of need, been my incredibly vital support system and who modeled the strength that has gotten me where I am. Aunt Terry, Aunt Kate, and Aunt Jeanie, a few sentences here aren't enough to say "Thank You" for your inspiration and for being such powerful successful, Hall-of-Fame female role models. You've allowed me to escape to your each of your houses countless times, and stepped in throughout my life to save me from myself, to help me heal, to pick me up. Undoubtedly, ReRe is grateful for all you have done to care for me and the girls since her passing. I hope this book is up to the HOF standards you have set, it sure is a high bar! My gratitude needs to be mentioned to those faith-filled women who are a part my heritage and came before them as well, including my grandmother, Mom Mom or "the fun Marie" as I knew her, and my Babci. Both women always put family first and Babci I will always remember for her dedication to prayer, while I hold close to my heart Mom Mom's trademark sense of humor and quick wit. I will never fire any of you.

I'm eternally grateful to Jeff and Carolann Scott, aka Mom and Dad 2. Thank you for showing me grace and forgiveness after my acting so recklessly and treating those close to me so terribly. My eleven-plus years of sobriety has been made possible in large part because you allowed me the time to pick myself back up, but more importantly because once amends were made you allowed me to prove to you that I had turned things around. Never once have you made me carry any shame and guilt like a black cloud or heavy weight. Your willingness to re-embrace me after causing so much pain played an integral role in my ability to remain sober. Your love and support over the years remain at the top of my gratitude list. Who would have thought that this Wednesday girl would have put you through so much? But hopefully, the ups have outweighed the downs. I'm delighted that we are living closer now and that the girls are able to have you as such a big part of their lives. Pop Pop, thank you for making me feel proud of myself, feeling like I am doing a good job with the girls, and for always having words of wisdom to share with me. Oma, thank you for all your advice when it comes to developing Reagan as an artist. She is so very lucky to have a personal art instructor and it is amazing to watch her blossom as an artist thanks to your guidance. I may provide the materials, but you have the wisdom and talent that I most definitely lack.

A big shout out to my best big brother, Broseph/Joseph, and Rali not only for helping out with car pools while working full time yourselves, but also for your love and moving so close. You have been essential in getting me through the toughest of times, especially when I was feeling stranded and helpless both physically and emotionally. It's wonderful to see the cousins grow up together, enriching each other's lives and getting to celebrate more family holidays together without travel impediments. ReRe/Mom probably told us millions of times when we were growing up "If you don't have anything nice to say, don't say anything at all." Well, bro - look how far (or close!) we've come. I know she is smiling down on us as we reinforce the importance of family and faith first.

A note of appreciation in abundance to my inherited brothers and sisters, Dan, Charlene, Marianne, Jason, Kevin and Nicole. You have shown me that having a lot of siblings is awesome, because you are all so supportive. And sarcastic and silly too, naturally. Having a big family means never needing to look far for a friend, a shoulder, a hug and, in this family *definitely* a laugh. I've needed you throughout and I thank you for each and every one of those hugs, the laughter, and for lending me your shoulders to cry on. I don't know how I would have gotten through it all without you. I had peace during the tough times knowing that you were of huge support to Jim and the girls as well. Thank you for all of your encouragement, kind hearts and helping hands.

In addition to my inherited siblings, my sincerest thank you to Mama Marta and Sweet Lou. You have not only told me you love me like one of your own, but genuinely treated me like one. I've shed more than a few tears on both of your shoulders and bent your ears with my woes over the years and I'm so blessed by your endearing and always encouraging presence in my life. Your words of wisdom during our ever-amusing kitchen chats (right Char?) while doing dishes at holidays are treasured. With this extended family, the holiday chaos is worthwhile because we have each other and our time together is priceless. Love all of you!

A heartfelt thank you to Beautiful Susan, who checks on me like a second mother and who I know would drop everything in a heartbeat like an on-call physician to take care of me and my family if ever necessary. You make me smile every time you call and I have needed every single one of the belly laughs you've provided throughout the years. Your ability to recount infamous ReRe shenanigans that I can no longer recall has preciously kept her spirit and memory alive for me. I am grateful for your love and encouragement always.

My heartfelt thanks to Dr. Hershenberg for helping Jim and me repave our road and put our family back on track. You have put so many valuable tools in our toolbox over the years and helped us tremendously with your levelheaded guidance, honesty, and wisdom. It is because of the work you have done with us that we have been able to navigate the twists and turns of this path with only minor potholes needing repairs every now and again instead of needing to put up signs saying, "Road Permanently Closed." I am forever grateful. Our family would not be what it is today if not for you, and this book certainly would not have been possible, either.

I would like to recognize my immense level of appreciation for and thanks to the Sisters of Mercy. Your perpetual prayers from far and wide have helped our entire family get through the hardest of times, especially after Mom's passing. It is because of your vigilance in prayer on my behalf that I probably have a special panel of angels on-call specifically for my medical issues and complications. I am forever indebted to you and would not have been able to write this book without role models of faith like you and your dedication to the mission of Catherine McAuley. I can only hope to repay you all someday with my service in turn, and I pray that God blesses you all and grants you the same health and happiness that you all have prayed for me over the years.

As another particularly influential role model in faith, I'd like to thank the best bear-hug giver and our treasured guest wedding speaker, Brother Brian Henderson. Your signature booming voice has articulated countless (and I do mean countless) words of wisdom over the years, most especially in regards to patience and practicing kindness with myself. Perhaps it is no coincidence that Jim and I have successfully navigated our broken road because you were the one who blessed it from the start, reminding us that "love is everything". You have played an integral role in helping me see the "big picture" of faith and life as it swirls about and especially during the most faith testing of times. True to form, you are always able to give me a boost with your Brother Brian-ism's, "As Ever's", and of course, your continuous prayer.

To the staff at Chesterbrook, including Eileen, Carol and most especially Amber and Kristen. You went above and beyond in my times of need. I couldn't have asked for a better learning environment for Julia and emotional support for Reagan, but what an added bonus to gain a meaningful friendship and such considerate cheerleaders in the process. You are all grossly underpaid for the amount of heart and overtime you put forth outside the classroom and I wouldn't have my sanity intact if not for how much help you all provided. And being left without sanity, I would never have started or seen this book through to completion, so I thank you all! Amber, you especially leave me in awe. While I might be stronger than I ever knew possible, I've never seen anyone with your juggling skills, Sista. You go from being supermom to your own remarkable young man, to having the gargantuan responsibility of managing the development of other people's children at multiple schools in the district. Then you go work on your own degree, only to strap on your goggles for the home gig as contractor/renovator! I can't believe you were ever able to fit helping me out in there somewhere. My gratitude can only be repaid to you with more Phillies experiences, gorgeous.

To my BGF, Theresa, I guess my life would be entirely different and perhaps this book might exist at all if not for your matchmaking skills, eh?? So, thank you my dear! We may not see each other as often as we would like these days because life keeps getting in the way. But I won't be saying bye bye bye anytime soon because you're just a phone call away, and I'll be loving you (forever), no strings attached. You know where to find me, I'll keep hangin' tough no matter what. I'm beyond grateful for our practically lifelong friendship and would be on a totally different path if not for that fateful phone call you made to Jim on my behalf. I'd like to think Jim and I would have found each other eventually because God has a funny way of making these things happen, but thank you for stepping in to make it happen a little quicker. No one else comes close to you, TP. You have stuck with me through thick and thin and every boy band concert in between. And that makes you larger than life!

To my 210 ladies, hard to believe we've been through twenty-plus years of friendship, because we are definitely *not* that old. Too many inside jokes for these pages (right, Sarah?) So I will simply say your friendship is priceless. If not for the High/Low emails as a resource I might not have been able to piece together much of the timeline contained in these pages, so thank you for your indirect help in making this possible! Despite the time that passes between communications (what is this thing called life that gets in the way, anyway??) it is incredible that our friendship has lasted this long and I cannot wait for the next reunion. Thank you for always giving me the boosts I need when I need them, you are all too far, indeed.

I have not by any means forgotten my Upstate NY network of angels. So many people displayed acts of kindness big and small and came to my aide during the surgeries and recovery. Whether it be making meals, delivering groceries, carpooling the kids, or just keeping me company. You definitely helped keep me sane by getting me around in those 9 months of winter. Miss Mary, you are the consummate example of a faith-filled survivor in my view. I still reflect fondly on our time together, every morning in fact, as I read my Jesus Calling passage. I am so grateful for your mentorship, your service, your love and your prayers.

A particular note of gratitude to our favorite Miss Laura and Miss Sue for taking care of me and the girls on many occasions. Neither of you ever hesitated to help when asked even though you had your own busy lives to manage. My life is richer because of the time I got to spend with you both. I wouldn't have been able to overcome all of the obstacles and hospital stays without your friendship and kindnesses.

To the staff and program at Seabrook House, the program that provided me the opportunity to get my life, my sobriety, and my family back: You are offering an amazing gift on your campus. I am blessed to be a successful "graduate," and I am eternally grateful for the lessons learned and time spent in your care. Thank you, favorite Aunt Kate, for finding and coordinating admission to the program. Without you, or the program who knows how this whole journey would have played out. I certainly wouldn't have acquired the skills I'd later need to be able to adjust and handle each curveball thrown.

To my rad right-hand-man, Adam for his editing work on this *genuinely* amazing piece of work. I'm ready to run for president of the Adam fan club for sure, and I do believe I owe you, per our contract, a parade upon publication! From our very first conversation I knew we would get along fabulously and that you were going to be the best guy to help bring this dream of mine to fruition. I've enjoyed working with you not just from the technical writing perspective because I feel like you've taught me a lot about myself in this cathartic process, as you bring such a deep spirituality to our conversations that I have connected with and can appreciate. Also, your ability to cite Bible quotes or name the Chapter/Verse of source of one on demand is astonishing. To then balance your spiritual depth of knowledge with a quick-witted sense of humor, and having that black belt in response time, you've just got it all. I have *truly* enjoyed working with you and I am so *stoked* about this finished project. You are a rad human, bro. I'll miss ya.

And to all of you, unnamed but otherwise known in my heart for providing your everlasting love and prayers when needed, most especially during my surgeries and recovery. My world may have seemed like it was crashing down at times and I felt too weak to carry on. All I had to do was look over my shoulder and I could always find someone standing there to get me through the seemingly impossible times. Whether it be an angel, God, extended family, a best good friend, or a loved one – I need not look far to find love was all around.

Brain damaged and all, I will never forget those who contributed to lifting me up, having my back and lessening my load. To those who have brightened my days just with a text or call of support throughout, I cannot express on these pages or even another 908 just like 'em how instrumental your presence has been and continues to be. While (let's hope) I've gotten through the worst of things, I still welcome customary check-ins, of course!

If you made it to the very last paragraph, my generous reader, with seatbelt intact, I hope you enjoyed the drive. Whatever tomorrow brings, God willing, I'll be here with open arms ready for the unwritten chapters to unfold. I'll be sending my love, positivity and prayers for your own health and happiness back out into the universe as a token of my thanks to all of you. I am only here, and this book was only made possible because of everyone's encouragement, kindness, caring shoulders, and many prayers. *Thank you, truly, with gratitude.*

Made in the USA
Columbia, SC
09 March 2024